AMERICA ON THE EVE OF THE CIVIL WAR

AMERICA

★ ON THE EVE OF THE ★

CIVIL WAR

Edited by Edward L. Ayers *and* Carolyn R. Martin

Ex libris

The
Cauffield
Family

University of Virginia Press / Charlottesville and London

University of Virginia Press
Printed in the United States of America on acid-free paper

First published 2010

9 8 7 6 5 4 3 2 1

LIBRARY OF CONGRESS CATALOGING-IN-PUBLICATION DATA

America on the eve of the Civil War / edited by Edward L. Ayers and
Carolyn R. Martin.
   p.   cm.
   Includes bibliographical references and index.
   The first in a series of annual Signature Conferences sponsored by the Virginia
Sesquicentennial of the American Civil War Commission, "America on the Eve of
the Civil War" was held in April 2009.
   ISBN 978-0-8139-3063-3 (cloth : alk. paper)
   1. United States—History—1849–1877. 2. United States—Social conditions—
19th century. 3. United States—Census, 1860. 4. United States—Population—
History—19th century. 5. Southern States—Economic conditions—19th century.
6. Slavery—Economic aspects—Southern States—History—19th century. 7. Harpers
Ferry (W. Va.)—History—John Brown's Raid, 1859. 8. Presidents—United States—
Election—1860. 9. United States—Politics and government—1857–1861. I. Ayers,
Edward L., 1953– II. Martin, Carolyn R.
   E436.A47 2010
   973.7′11—dc22   2010010316

This book is published in association with the Virginia
Sesquicentennial of the American Civil War Commission
(www.VirginiaCivilWar.org).

CONTENTS

Acknowledgments

This book came out of a daylong conversation among sixteen superb historians. Their decades of scholarship equipped them for far-ranging and fascinating conversations, and we are grateful to each one who took on this challenge.

The conference would not have been possible without the vision and support provided by the Virginia Sesquicentennial of the American Civil War Commission: Speaker William J. Howell and Senator Charles J. Colgan Sr., chair and vice chair, respectively, and members of the commission, along with the very capable leadership of Ms. Cheryl L. Jackson, executive director.

Leaders of departments across the University of Richmond developed a finely tuned operations plan for hosting this event, and they carried it out with precision and enthusiasm. Members of "Team Sesqui," as they called themselves, were Roger Brooks, Elizabeth Chenery, Bettie Clarke, Tim Coates, Linda Evans, John Jacobs, Jim Morris, Carla Shriner, and Doug West. Dave DeBarger and Craig Keeton of Richmond public television station WCVE and Dan Yeary of BVC, working with the university's telecom, multimedia, and network services professionals, delivered an exceptional experience to those on site and joining us via the Web.

Members of our university campus community—staff, faculty, students, and alumni—rallied to make this a memorable event for our guests, from serving as hosts and shuttle drivers, preparing lunches, setting up exhibit stations, managing registrations, selling books, and conducting interviews, to processing questions from the Robins Center audience and those around the world.

We are especially grateful for the careful review, fact checking, and editing of Philip Herrington, Kenny Marotta, and Ruth Melville. Their work helped shape the transcript of our daylong conversation into the book before you.

Edward L. Ayers, conference chair
Carolyn R. Martin, chair, "Team Sesqui"

1859 Chronology

JANUARY 7 Prospector George A. Jackson makes the first substantial discovery of gold near what would become Idaho Springs, Colorado, sparking an influx of miners to the area.

FEBRUARY 14 Oregon becomes the 33rd state of the Union.

MARCH 2–3 The sale of 436 enslaved people belonging to Pierce Butler of Philadelphia—reputed to be the largest slave auction in American history—takes places in Savannah, Georgia.

JULY 18 Representatives of the largely non-Mormon mining residents of the western portion of Utah Territory meet to create a Declaration of Cause for Separation in an attempt to establish a separate Nevada Territory. The silver-bearing Comstock Lode is discovered that summer. Nevada Territory is finally established in 1861.

SEPTEMBER 5 The first African American novel published in the United States, *Our Nig, or Sketches from the Life of a Freed Black,* by Harriet Wilson, begins production through Rand & Avery of Boston.

OCTOBER 4 Kansas voters approve the antislavery Wyandotte Constitution by a margin of two to one.

OCTOBER 16 John Brown leads a raid on the Federal arsenal at Harpers Ferry, Virginia, in an attempt to take over Virginia state government and spark a widespread slave rebellion in the South.

OCTOBER 17 Army Brevet Colonel Robert E. Lee and a company of Marines sent by President James Buchanan surround the Harpers Ferry engine house taken over by John Brown and his men.

OCTOBER 18 After U.S. Marines charge the engine house, John Brown is severely wounded and arrested.

OCTOBER 24   Settlers in modern-day Colorado establish the Provisional Government of the Territory of Jefferson, never recognized by the United States government. The official Territory of Colorado replaced it in 1861.

OCTOBER 31   The trial of John Brown begins at Charles Town, Jefferson County, Virginia.

NOVEMBER 28   American author and historian Washington Irving dies in Tarrytown, New York.

DECEMBER 2   John Brown is hanged in Charles Town.

America on the Eve of the Civil War

INTRODUCTION

EDWARD L. AYERS

No one was sure what to expect. Sixteen historians from varying backgrounds and perspectives were coming together to talk about one of the most controversial topics in American history for an entire day. They would not invoke anything that happened after the end of 1859, a restraint possible because they knew their subject so well they understood what they could *not* have known at that time. And they were doing this in front of two thousand people from all over the United States and on streaming video.

The scholarship and public history the sixteen historians had created over their careers made this plan seem at least feasible. Their collective body of work embraced everything from politics to literature, from industrial slavery to African American art, from women's reform efforts to racial ideologies, from military history to the history of memory. Some of them worked at museums and libraries while others taught at universities and colleges across the nation. They belonged to no particular school of interpretation, and quite a few had never met one another.

The historians, whatever their backgrounds, shared a sense of responsibility for opening a national conversation about the causes, events, and consequences of the American Civil War on its 150th anniversary. When the Virginia Sesquicentennial Commission approached the University of Richmond to see if we might be interested in hosting the first session to wrestle with the commemoration, we jumped at the chance. The former capital of the Confederacy and a center of the internal slave trade would be a fitting place to begin the conversation about the meaning of the Civil War and the end of slavery.

When they approached us, the representatives of the commission asked, logically enough, if we would host that first session on the "coming of the Civil War." Despite our general enthusiasm, we warned that those words, so obvious and commonsensical, actually hinder our understanding of the war. They rush the story along, waste too much information, foreclose too many ways of seeing how the Civil War embodied the full scope of American history. If, instead, the session explored the years before the conflict began, ranging broadly across the entire continent and embracing all Americans, it would better explain how the war, as Abraham Lincoln would later put it, "came." We could better see what we were looking for if we broadened our scope of vision.

The commission's leaders enthusiastically embraced that notion, and we proceeded to frame a conversation around America on the eve of the Civil War. A better name, we noted, would have been "America on what would become the eve of the Civil War," but that was more than a mouthful. The participants in the conversation signed on to the concept of invoking nothing after December 31, 1859. Several conference calls wrestled with that premise and its consequences, and the more we talked, the more interesting the idea became. We would begin our analysis with what the historical actors, the people who actually made the history, knew and believed. The restricted perspective was not a gimmick but a challenging discipline. Like a detective who searches for the motivations for a crime in clues that do not seem obvious at first, the historians in this conversation did not dwell only on the obvious issues that moved the nation. Things that did not seem immediately related to the war turned out to be crucial.

The refusal to look ahead allowed us to set aside some of the usual conventions of Civil War discussion. "No one secedes; in fact, the Confederacy does not exist," my opening remarks warned those who had journeyed from twenty-six states to join us in a large basketball arena at the University of Richmond. "Robert E. Lee will play a lead role, but in command of *United States* troops at Harpers Ferry. Tom Jackson is still a math professor at VMI, though he will lead cadets to ensure order at the hanging of John Brown at the very end of the year. Sam Grant is a bill collector in St. Louis, and 'Cump' Sherman is heading up a military school in Louisiana. Jefferson Davis is still a United States senator and Abraham Lincoln is a successful lawyer and a failed senatorial candidate with good prospects." Richmond itself was in 1859 "a booming modern city, full of immigrants, free black people, and factories." After encouraging and insightful remarks from Governor Timothy Kaine and the head of the Sesquicentennial Commission, Speaker of the House William Howell, we plunged into the discussion.

For most of 1859, it turned out, only one year before the momentous election of 1860, little happened that would have told Americans that they were living on the precipice of a continent-wide war and the end of the most powerful slave society in the world. Republicans widely distributed Hinton Rowan Helper's *The Impending Crisis,* which had come out two years earlier, arguing that slavery damaged, economically and politically, the non-slaveholding white majority in the South. The book helped mobilize Republicans, who were gaining ground in Northern states on the divided Democrats, but the putative audience for the book—white men in the South who owned no slaves—ignored or derided it. The most salient features of politics in 1859 were the obvious weakness and corruption of the Buchanan administration. That was why the Republicans were looking for someone who could be trumpeted as honest. A man from outside the usual circuits of power and dealing would be ideal.

The truly electrifying event of 1859 would be John Brown's raid at Harpers Ferry, Virginia, in October. That raid was so profoundly unexpected, so complicated in its origins and in its consequences, that Americans at the time hardly knew what to make of it. The response was paradoxical, with most white Northerners apparently agreeing at the outset with all white Southerners that Brown was, at best, insane. The long delay between the raid and his execution in December, however, gave Brown an opportunity to frame the issues so that he became a martyr. Though the Republicans kept their distance from Brown, white Southerners blamed the Republicans in any case. America in 1859 was a hall of mirrors in which people fought reflections of reflections.

Gary Gallagher got a good laugh, and made a key point, when he pointed out that few white people woke up in the mornings of 1859 and thought first about the sectional crisis. Fittingly, therefore, the first session of the day focused on the things that people did think about, including the vast immigration from Ireland and Germany. This immigration fed growth, uncertainty, and conflict in American religion and in the American economy, in the cities and the countryside. Millions of newly arrived people, the men among them voting not long after coming to the United States, fed resentment and fear among many who were already here. Nativism fueled the Know-Nothing Party, which in turn helped destroy what remained of the Whigs and fed into the nascent Republican Party.

The breakneck expansion of the nation, the product of countless individual decisions fed by ambition, desperation, calculation, and sheer restlessness, became another major thread of discussion. "The territories" became a critical stage for the conflicts that fed the Civil War, but political consequence played little role in the thinking of the people who moved. Their migration put the nation and the Constitution under enormous strain over the issue of slavery, but that did not factor into the calculations of many families. Whether in Missouri in 1820, Texas in 1845, California in 1850, or Kansas in 1854, a flood of people moving west drove political struggle back east.

Railroads and telegraphs, we heard in the opening conversation, transformed one area of life after another. The race to the West would not have been nearly as rapid, as large, or as momentous for those left behind had it not been for the railroads that connected the nation in the 1840s and 1850s. The economic life of the country, in every region, in manufacturing, agriculture, and slavery, surged because of new means of transportation. The nation suddenly found itself tied together in new ways, and that very unification created the conditions that led to its disunion. The events in Kansas, Harpers Ferry, and even Washington, D.C., could not have electrified the entire United States without the instantaneous spread of news fed by a burgeoning partisan press driven by the telegraph.

The changes in immigration, population, politics, transportation, and communication help explain why it was that slavery, which had been a national presence for more than two centuries before 1859, suddenly became so combustible. For the nonhistorians in attendance at the conference, perhaps the largest single surprise was the strength of slavery on the eve of the Civil War. People have long been taught that slavery was weakening. Some of that interpretation is a holdover from older pro-Southern arguments that war was not necessary because slavery would have faded away in its own time. Other assumptions about the weakness of slavery come from exactly the opposite direction, a holdover from Republican arguments that slavery was backward and incompatible with economic growth. Those two older currents converged in the familiar argument that the Civil War was a fight between the "industrial" North and the "agrarian" South, a formulation that became popular in the 1920s in the work of Charles and Mary Beard and that has shown remarkable durability.

The Richmond conference, especially the session on the future of the South, showed how misleading that common interpretation is. The North was not nearly as dominated by cities and factories as our collective imagination portrays it, and the slave South was far more integrated into the world of business, finance, manufacturing, insurance, technology, and international trade than many people imagine. When Charles Dew projected a page from the account book of the Richmond slave broker Hector Davis on the large screen in the auditorium, people gasped when they saw that this one businessman had conducted transactions in the sale of men, women, and children of over two and a half million dollars in 1859 alone.

The slave trade in Richmond was far larger than this, of course, enveloping a considerable portion of the central business district. And that trade was growing throughout the 1850s, gathering and shipping tens of thousands of people every month from across the Middle Atlantic states to New Orleans and Texas. Many merchants, bankers, and suppliers who did not deal in slaves directly built businesses around their trade with the slave traders. The enslaved people who lived in Richmond worked in some quite modern occupations, ranging from iron and tobacco to flour and tourism.

African American people were a central presence in the future capital of the Confederacy, involved in every aspect of the city's life and economy. They sustained their own churches, lived in their own neighborhoods, and regularly made attempts at escape and freedom. But there was nothing about the evolution of slavery itself, other than its dismaying economic strength and geographic expansion, that fed the conflict between the North and the South. White Southerners hardly lashed out in desperation over a dying institution. If anything, they were too confident in the future of slavery, too certain that the nation's economy depended on the vast profits of the cotton and other goods produced by slavery, too sure that the industrialized world would stumble and fall without the bounty produced by the enslaved people of the South. When Walter Johnson argued that white Southerners viewed Cuba and Latin America as lands ripe for the expansion of American slavery, people in the audience were taken aback, their frame of reference suddenly expanded.

The discussion of politics proved just as surprising. The historians unraveled a remarkably complex series of personalities, accidents, and structural changes that brought the United States to the fractured, unstable, and unpredictable political situation of 1859. Long-term developments such as westward expansion, immigration, and the spread of the telegraph fed the instability, but so did volatile events that dominated the newspapers. The attack on Massachusetts senator Charles Sumner by South Carolina representative Preston Brooks dramatized the growing resentment between the North and the South, inflaming regional fears and fantasies. News from Bleeding Kansas kept the wounds raw for month after month, turning the actions of a relatively few people into a morality play for the nation.

By themselves, these episodes might have come and gone. Had the Democrats not been weakened by President James Buchanan's passivity and reputation for surrounding himself with corrupt cronies, had Buchanan and the powerful senator Stephen A. Douglas been able to come to terms, had the Whigs not faded away after their loss of long-time leaders and defining purpose, had the Know-Nothings been able to sustain their sudden rise to power, and had the Republicans not turned to more moderate leaders, the flamboyant dramas of regional conflict might have passed in 1860, as they had so often before. But an election was looming in 1860 and people on all sides jockeyed for advantage, recklessly playing with the nation's future for political advantage. By the end of 1859, the dangers of that jockeying were not yet apparent. The candidates for the next year's election, including Abraham Lincoln, were by no means evident, and neither was the strange four-way contest that would soon pull the nation apart.

The four conversations that make up this book remind us that people lived economic, religious, and cultural history at the same time they lived political and ideological history. History is unpredictable not merely because surprising events occur but because every part of history impinges on every other part. Everything constantly moves and everything constantly touches everything else. Our familiar stories of the Civil War isolate regional conflict from all the other things going on that pulled in different directions. The conversations in this book, in contrast, offer a much more dynamic view of history, taking more Americans and more kinds of Americans into account.

It was, frankly, surprising that such a coherent view of this period emerged from the conversations in Richmond. The historians at the conference certainly brought different perspectives with them, and the format encouraged them to jostle with one another. But while they emphasized different topics and interpretations, they were surprised to find that they agreed on so much. The conversation revealed, in fact, that a new interpretation of the Civil War era has emerged from the last twenty-five years of scholarship. African American history, women's history, and immigrant history have flourished for decades now, with one breakthrough after another. Struggle, change, and complexity now dominate where broad generalization once characterized the representation of these people in our history books.

Detailed studies of political development, too, have shown the limitations of simplicity. Sophisticated studies of electoral patterns reveal that the constituencies of the Republicans and Democrats cannot be traced as simply as we once thought, that complex currents flowed into the new Republican Party. Studies of the South show that slaveholders often sought to protect slavery by protecting the Union and opposing secession. Histories of both the North and the South reveal how quickly things were changing in the late 1850s, how uncertain the prospects were for the most powerful men.

Economic history, too, has undergone radical change. Where not so long ago simple ideas of development, industrialization, and modernization dominated our understanding of economic life, historians now understand that economic change is anything but straightforward. There is hardly one path to economic development and that path does not invariably proceed through democracy and freedom. Studies of slavery in the United States and elsewhere reveal that forced labor can be fused with innovative forms of finance, transportation, communication, and political development. As historians come to understand the interrelations of national and international commerce, it becomes ever clearer that economic development knit the North and the South together ever more tightly and tied the South into complex webs of economic development far from its borders.

Dichotomies that long dominated American history have dissolved even though we do not yet have an account of the Civil War era that incorporates all the new dynamic elements. This slender book, in fact, may offer a glimpse into the history that is to come. The historians who gathered in Richmond did not come together to promote a new perspective on the defining conflict in American history. They would certainly not consider themselves a school. But each brought some particular perspective, some unique knowledge, to the conversation and revealed that our understanding of the American Civil War is growing richer, more inclusive, and more supple than we may have realized.

As we began the day, I asked a rhetorical question of the unexpectedly large audience in the arena where we met: "Why would you come as far as many of you have, and spend as much time as you seem prepared to spend, to discuss the years before any of the famous events of election, secession, war, emancipation, and reconstruction have occurred?" We already knew the answers from the hundreds of replies to the questions that we posted on the Web site where the participants registered. As I reminded them that day, they told us they were coming to Richmond "to help us reckon with the hardest parts of American history to comprehend. You have come here to help us think through the meanings of slavery, of violence, of nation, and of history itself. You have come here because you know that if we do not lay the foundations for our understanding of the Civil War in the 1840s and 1850s, there is no understanding the 1860s and 1870s." The people who journeyed to the former capital of the Confederacy to explore the years on the eve of the Civil War "know that if we do not understand the Civil War, we cannot understand the decades in the 150 years since, including our own. You have come here to show that Americans are ready, even hungry, to examine the Civil War on its 150th anniversary with fresh eyes."

David Blight, a participant at the conference, wrote a telling essay soon after the event. A student of the memory of the Civil War, Blight was struck by the difference between this conversation and those of the war's centennial fifty years earlier. American life changed profoundly over those decades and so has our understanding of the American past.

This book ends with Blight's thoughtful words because they remind us of what is at stake in our conversations about the American Civil War. If we come to that era ready to learn all that it can teach us, we can see ourselves, our past, and our many potential futures with a new and broader vision.

Opening Remarks

The first session was preceded by words of welcome from the Honorable William J. Howell, Speaker of the Virginia House of Delegates and head of the Virginia Sesquicentennial of the American Civil War Commission, and from the Governor of the Commonwealth, the Honorable Timothy M. Kaine.

SPEAKER HOWELL Good morning. Thank you very much, Dr. Ayers, for your leadership in chairing this first signature conference. The country's finest Civil War historians are assembled here today, including our host and conference chair, and we're looking forward to the innovative program that you all have worked so hard to develop. It's good to have so many people here with us today for this program, the first major sesquicentennial event in the country. People are here today from every corner of Virginia, and twenty-six other states, and many more are joining by webcast and through blogs. On behalf of the commission, I'd like to extend a warm welcome to each of you. And we're especially pleased to welcome today Governor Kaine and members of his cabinet, members of the Virginia General Assembly, Richmond city leaders, members of the commission's advisory council, work groups and local sesquicentennial committees throughout Virginia; teachers, classes joining us by webcast; and hosts of our upcoming signature conferences. And there are many here that have traveled a long distance to be with us, and we thank you for coming, and we're very glad that you're here.

It all begins here in Virginia, where, over the next six years, we plan to commemorate the 150th anniversary of the Civil War through programs that invite diversity, inclusiveness, and educational exploration. We'll take a multifaceted, comprehensive approach that addresses the Civil War from the viewpoints of the battlefront and the home front, that includes Union, Confederate, and African-American perspectives, and that looks at the cultural and social lessons of the war as well as the military lessons.

We will encourage preservation, preservation of lands and battlefields, of course, but also preservation of documents and records that give us first-person accounts of life during the Civil War. We'll also use technology to expand our reach and include new audiences. There's going to be something for everyone. That is why Virginia's commemoration begins now in 2009, while other states are just starting to think about the sesquicentennial. Much of their planning is focused on 2011, the anniversary of the first battles. And we will certainly remember those tragic engagements as well, but we will also look at the causes of the war, just as we're doing here today, and its enduring legacies.

As Dr. Ayers has said, today begins a national conversation, one that we hope will set a new tone and last for years to come. Virginia is proud to serve as the leader of the sesquicentennial, and we're glad that you're here today to experience it with us. Now it is my deep pleasure to introduce to you Timothy M. Kaine, governor of the Commonwealth of Virginia.

GOVERNOR KAINE   Thank you very much. Good morning and welcome to all who traveled for this wonderful program to kick off Virginia's analysis and commemoration of the sesquicentennial. I want to thank my friend Bill Howell for his kind words of introduction, and also for his leadership of the commission. Bill Howell, the Speaker of the House, is a great preservationist in many ways, but his effort to make sure that Virginia will discuss and commemorate the sesquicentennial has been a great public service, one of many that he's performed. I also want to congratulate Ed Ayers, the president of the University of Richmond, for putting on the program and bringing together such a great group of individuals.

Ed mentioned that the Civil War is the pivotal event in American history, but I would say, as a nonhistorian, that I can think of two: the Civil War and World War II. The Civil War forged our national identity to today, and World War II cemented our place as a dynamic force in bringing peace to the world. And these are related events. In Virginia and in America, William Faulkner's statement "History isn't dead, it's not even past" is very true as we think about the Civil War in Virginia. Just in my fifteen-year career in public office, I've been engaged in controversies and disputes about the placement of a statue of Arthur Ashe on Monument Avenue; the renaming of bridges that were once named for Civil War generals for Civil Rights veterans; the placement of the mural of Robert E. Lee on the flood wall in a display of murals in downtown Richmond; and the placement of the statue of Abraham Lincoln at the American Civil War Center in Richmond. All created controversy because people had different thoughts about the figures and the period represented therein. And then the Speaker and I have worked very hard together on Civil War battlefield preservation, preserving in the last few years all or parts of twenty-four different Civil War battlefield sites in Virginia. This conflict 150 years ago is not in the past. We are still wrestling with it today, as a commonwealth and as a country. And that's as it should be because this was a pivotal time in forging the identity of our country. Not only was the Civil War the war that ended slavery, the Civil War enabled civil government to go forward in a way that it wouldn't have otherwise.

I just finished reading a biography of Andrew Jackson and was surprised to learn that when Andrew Jackson was president there was a near secession battle of South Carolina, again, over issues of North versus South and slavery. Had the Civil War never been fought, and had the nation not come together, our ability to be a leader among nations would never have come to pass. Now by talking about these things, I'm violating the rule that today we're in 1859. But it is clearly the case that if America hadn't come together following the Civil War, through much pain and sacrifice and tragedy, we would not have been able to play the role that Lincoln foresaw. At the end of his second inaugural address, he said we should try to bind up the nation's wounds and achieve a just and lasting peace among ourselves and among all nations. The United States would not have been able to play the wonderful role we've been able to play among all nations had we not bound up our wounds and come together at the end of the Civil War. As we learn today from great scholars and participate in the panel discussions in an interactive way, we are not just commemorating something that happened 150 years ago, but we are taking lessons from it that we can use to continue to move forward as a nation.

About a month ago, the Speaker and I were at the ceremony commemorating the preservation of a battlefield site in Fredericksburg, part of the battle of Fredericksburg, Slaughter Pen Farm. At that occasion I had a thought that applies to this seminar as well. What we're doing today is giving life to an Old Testament phrase. You probably remember the injunction that we should beat swords into plowshares—a great kind of mystical phrase. We're taking a sword, a tragic history, a tragic moment in this nation's history where so many lives were shattered and altered and blood was shed, and we are turning it into a plowshare; namely, we are learning from it, we are gathering new insights so that we can again be that nation that is bound together peacefully among ourselves and peacefully with the nations of the world.

Thanks very much and I hope you have a great day.

Bird's-eye view of New Orleans, Louisiana, with the Mississippi River in the foreground; John Bachmann, artist, published by A. Guerber & Co., New York. (Library of Congress, Prints and Photographs Division)

1 Taking Stock of the Nation in 1859

Presenters were Christy Coleman, Gary Gallagher, Walter Johnson, and Joan Waugh, with Edward L. Ayers moderating.

ED AYERS   We're talking about the era right before the Civil War. Later sessions will look at slavery in Virginia and Richmond, at John Brown's raid, and at the upcoming election of 1860. This session's presenters are going to paint a broad panorama of what the United States is like in the years coming up to the Civil War. It strikes me that these 1850s have been pretty interesting times. What do you think is going to leap out from the census that is being taken for the country? It will later be known as the 1860 census, but it was actually taken in 1859.

GARY GALLAGHER   I think growth is going to be one remarkable thing, growth in many, many ways: Growth in the expansion of a transportation and information network with the railroad and the telegraph. Expansion in population. The country is growing unbelievably quickly in terms of how many people live here. And immigration. I think the dominant theme is growth and energy.

JOAN WAUGH   Immigration has been remarkable. The two largest immigrant groups coming into the United States, mostly into the Northern states, are the Germans and Irish. In thinking about how to answer this question, I looked at just one city, St. Louis, Missouri. Is Missouri a western state? Is it a Southern state? Is it a Northern state? The answer is all three. If we look at St. Louis, we see that it has a population of 167,000 in 1859, with 60,000 immigrants from Germany and 39,000 from Ireland, making it an incredibly diverse city, and perhaps explaining why, in the late 1850s, an antislavery mayor was elected in that growing and prosperous port city.

ED AYERS Do any enslaved people live there?

JOAN WAUGH Very few. Ten percent of the general population in Missouri is enslaved, down 2 percent from the previous census, but the enslaved population living in St. Louis is very small.

CHRISTY COLEMAN The influx of Germans and Irish, in particular, is not only shaping the growth of these communities but also having an impact on the social environment. They are picking up their possessions, which are very limited, and coming into these Northern cities looking for work. They're often being placed in work environments that are just deplorable. There's no other way to say it. Women and children and men are working in deplorable factory conditions.

The other thing that is striking is that they're also beginning to be pitted against African Americans, whether enslaved or free. The newspapers and all of those wonderful little illustrated booklets are developing caricatures that put African Americans and Irish literally on the same scale, showing that they are somehow equal socially. You see the two biting at each other. And they do. There are a lot of conflicts between these two groups as they are trying to find their place in society. As we think about these numbers, there's also a social dynamic. The Germans, Brits, Scots, and others are coming here with some means and are able to acquire land, solidify themselves in a community, and make themselves a part of the political fabric, something that the Irish are not able to do at the same level.

ED AYERS Do the Irish and Germans live in the same places? Where do they tend to migrate to?

CHRISTY COLEMAN Again, the Irish are pretty much going into the Northern cities, the larger Northern cities. We're seeing them in Boston, Philadelphia, and New York. The Germans tend to head farther west.

JOAN WAUGH Cincinnati is another place that they go. Chicago.

ED AYERS And Richmond.

GARY GALLAGHER There's a thriving German community in central Texas, in the hill country of Texas. There are pockets of immigrants in many places, predominantly north of the Ohio and the Potomac. But there are immigrants everywhere. New Orleans has a flourishing immigrant community, as does Charleston.

WALTER JOHNSON What you've seen over the 1850s that will also show up in the census is a massive relocation of enslaved people from the Upper South to the Lower South, about a quarter of a million people in the 1850s. The slave market is booming in the late 1850s, and that has a devastating impact on enslaved families in the Upper South. Forty percent of those relocations involve the separation of a family. The boom in the slave market also has implications for social relations among white people. By the 1850s slave prices are getting so high that it's becoming very, very difficult for non-slaveholding white people to buy slaves. By 1857, and quite critically by 1859, that is beginning to set up tension within the slaveholding South over the question of support by non-slaveholding white people for the institution of slavery. This massive relocation of slaves is setting up an intraregional dynamic between the Upper and Lower South, between places like Virginia and Mississippi and Louisiana. There's a fear that the booming cotton South in the late 1850s is going to drain so many enslaved people out of the Upper South that support for slavery in a state like Virginia will be attenuated.

GARY GALLAGHER I think the census will also show something else, and that is that Colorado might be next in line to be a state. It's possible, because there's been a tremendous amount of mining going on in Colorado, which had a great strike just last year in 1858.

ED AYERS A labor strike?

GARY GALLAGHER No, a strike of gold, a better kind of strike from the point of view of the people going west. They're going west, and they're going in very large numbers. The effect of that movement promises to rival what happened in California just ten or eleven years ago in terms of the wealth that's going to come out of that part of the Rocky Mountains. A great deal of wealth is heading east out of the mountains of Colorado, and it might work tremendously to benefit the nation as a whole.

ED AYERS It sounds like the economy is doing pretty well.

GARY GALLAGHER In some ways it is. Cotton exports are certainly thriving. But the nation has been through a very difficult economic patch just two years ago. More than five thousand businesses failed.

Now that the Crimean War is over, Russian wheat is coming back on the market, hurting our wheat farmers. I'd say it's a mixed picture economically.

JOAN WAUGH Actually, the South is doing better coming out of the depression of 1857 than the other regions of the country.

ED AYERS Why?

JOAN WAUGH Because the cotton economy is still booming.

ED AYERS It's like the oil of today. Cotton is much like that, isn't it? It's the big commodity of the world, and the South has a monopoly on it.

GARY GALLAGHER It gives the United States a favorable balance of trade all by itself. We export more cotton than everything else put together.

ED AYERS You talked before, Gary, about what the next state might be. What does the map of the United States look like right now?

WALTER JOHNSON I think the next state in 1859 might be Cuba. Let's set aside the notion that comes out of the history of the Civil War and imagine a conflict that's not defined by "seceding from" but the question of what it is that people think they are seceding to. One of the things that people, particularly in the Mississippi valley, believe that they are seceding to is a global commercial empire, founded on the power of cotton, founded on the fact that cotton is the leading sector in the global economy.

ED AYERS So people really think they might be able to add Cuba as a state?

WALTER JOHNSON It's the official policy of the United States government with the Ostend Manifesto in 1854, right? Until that becomes public, it's the secret policy of the United States government. Cuba is viewed as the lynchpin of the joining of the Mississippi valley economy to the Atlantic economy, and then potentially to the Pacific across the isthmus at Nicaragua or Panama. And the fear about Cuba is that Spanish colonial governments in Cuba are so weak that the British will take over Cuba. Actually, throughout the 1850s there's a very great emphasis, not simply among proslavery expansionists, but also among New York merchant capitalists and shipping interests, to annex Cuba to the United States.

JOAN WAUGH That relationship is also present in some of the more colorful stories of American expansionism during the 1850s, when private individuals led military expeditions to Mexico and to Nicaragua. One of the most famous of the so-called filibusters—"filibuster" in this case means somebody who decides he wants to be king or president of some country—was William Walker. Walker was born in Memphis, Tennessee, and was a doctor. He was a very restless man. He moved to New Orleans, became a lawyer and then a journalist. He then went to the California goldfields in San Francisco and later was working as a newspaper reporter when he just decided, "It's time for me to be king of Baja, California, and Sonora, Mexico." The Californians were on board. It was a very different state, very pro-Southern in some parts.

ED AYERS   They were looking for a king?

JOAN WAUGH   No, they had interests in northern Mexico. Walker went down there with about two hundred men and engaged in an unsuccessful attempt to control Baja, California, and Sonora, Mexico. The Mexican army escorted him out, and at the border the United States military arrested him and put him on trial in California for violating neutrality laws. He was acquitted. Then he went on to Nicaragua—which is another very colorful story—and he recruited five hundred men, mostly from California. The South was very interested and supportive of these filibustering measures, although it caused a little bit of trouble.

ED AYERS   How does that work out for him?

JOAN WAUGH   It doesn't work out well. He will be executed.

WALTER JOHNSON   But he became the president of Nicaragua.

GARY GALLAGHER   And he brought slavery to Nicaragua. He reopened the Atlantic slave trade. To come back to Walter's point about Cuba, Cuba has a lot to do with cotton, but it also has a lot to do, potentially, with power in our Senate because the slaveholding states are, frankly, losing power there. Only two slave states have come in since 1845, Florida and Texas, but five free states have come in: Iowa, Wisconsin, California, most recently Oregon, just this year, and Minnesota last year. Two times those numbers are how many new senators you get. It's very clear that the slaveholding states are losing power in the Senate. They've long since lost it in the House of Representatives, of course. Cuba holds the prospect of enhancing the slaveholding presence in the United States.

ED AYERS It sounds like this could be frustrating for Southern leaders. Their economy is the one that's booming, they have these international plans, and yet they're losing out in the United States Senate. Is that fueling some of this tension?

CHRISTY COLEMAN Absolutely. I think one of the things that we forget is that in the South we have a fixed way of thinking about our leadership. And that is steeped in history. The Founding Fathers are Virginians. There is a pride in being Southern, and there is a pride in the particular order that life should be. That pride is built on a sense of social superiority, particularly among whites, and a sense of the right to be in charge, quite frankly. A lot of people took the fact that the South was not hurt nearly as much in the depression of '57 as all those New York bankers as some kind of verification that the slave system of the South was the superior system on which to run.

We talk about this expansion. Yes, they're looking at social power and political power being lost, but there's another thing that's taking place that is equally dramatic. These abolitionists are a pain unlike any pain white Southerners of 1859 have dealt with. They are virulent in their work. They are aiding and abetting, trying to get black folks to run away from their kindly homes where they're taken care of. Why would they want to leave? Abolitionists are just troublemakers. They're interlopers. Why are they down here? This is the attitude of the majority of the white population.

Now, the small farmer generally could not care less. But we have to remember that the price of slaves is going up. At one point a person said, "Well, if I work this land and I make a little money, I can get myself a slave or two, and then I can begin my social climb." That is being impeded a bit because the prices are going so high, and African Americans are being moved farther south. You really are seeing this interesting shift, and people really are being challenged, and they don't like being challenged.

And then there are those Northern women who are running around, having all these conventions, talking about women's rights. Well, Southern women do not want to be referred to as women. They want to be referred to as ladies, and ladies are distinctly different. Forgive me for being tongue-in-cheek, but this is the social environment that we're dealing with. Southerners are seeing an attack on their social system, they're being challenged politically in terms of their clout and power as these new states are coming in. Their very way of life is being challenged. Meanwhile, African Americans are continuing to run. I mean, they are beating feet as fast as they can, heading across these borders, trying to get north. And you've got people up there in places like Philadelphia and Boston and Detroit that are helping them get to Canada, for crying out loud. They're stealing property.

GARY GALLAGHER   The best friend of the slaveholding South in that regard is the federal government. Increasingly the states and slaveholders of the South look to the United States government to ensure their hold on their property. They expect the entire nation to follow through with the legislation that came out of the Compromise of 1850 that said escaping slaves will be returned. State rights have been a problem from the Southern perspective in that many of the Northern states have passed laws that make it difficult to enforce federal law.

ED AYERS   So you're saying the South is favorable to federal power?

GARY GALLAGHER   That's exactly what I'm saying, because the federal government is its best friend. There are problematic state governments in a number of the Northern states that are trying to impose— to "interpose," to use a word that John C. Calhoun of South Carolina used—their power between the reach of the central government and runaway slaves.

ED AYERS   But it's also the case, is it not, that there are some in the North who help the federal government return slaves? The case of Anthony Burns stands out.

WALTER JOHNSON   With the fugitive slave laws, there's an autonomous administrative structure set up. It's administrative law. And it's a law that is independent of any sort of judicial oversight. The execution of that law is, I think, thoroughgoing in many cases. And the commissioners are paid twice as much when they determine that a given person, say, Anthony Burns, is a fugitive slave, rather than determining that Anthony Burns is a free person of color that somebody is trying to kidnap. [Anthony Burns, born a slave in Virginia, fled to Boston in 1853. When discovered in 1854, he was arrested and became an example of the federal government's resolve to enforce the Fugitive Slave Law of 1850, which required all slaves to be returned to their masters, regardless of where they were when discovered.] What one can see in the operation, then, is that the federal government is not simply involved in protecting the property rights of slaveholders—the so-called property rights of slaveholders—in the North, but it is also involved in what in other contexts would be called kidnapping, in taking free people of color and turning them, legally, into slaves in a place like Philadelphia. That's, in a sense, what happens. Now, what happens with Anthony Burns is that there is successful mob action on the part of antislavery Bostonians to rescue him from federal administrative action, although Burns, I believe, is later taken back to Virginia.

GARY GALLAGHER   The Pierce administration put its full weight behind returning Anthony Burns.

JOAN WAUGH   To add to this part of our discussion, beginning with Christy's description of the growing unease of Southern politicians and the Southern leadership structure about abolitionists over, if you will, bringing freedom out of the closet: In the North, perhaps abolitionists are not that popular, but their message is still being debated. There is a growing idea among Northerners, the vast majority of whom are not abolitionists, about a Slave Power conspiracy. Each side is getting a bit paranoid about the other. All the brouhaha around Anthony Burns's trial and the mob action is certainly a part of that. It's not enough that Southerners control and dominate the national government, the presidency, and the Congress. Now they want to come into our states and our cities and make us do things we don't want to do, things that we don't think are right.

ED AYERS   You mentioned that the vast majority of white Northerners were not abolitionists. Would you be willing to put any numbers on that, Joan, to give people a sense of proportion?

JOAN WAUGH   I would say probably 97 percent of white Northerners are not abolitionists.

ED AYERS   What defines an abolitionist?

JOAN WAUGH   There is a range. The abolitionists we think of are led by Frederick Douglass and William Lloyd Garrison, who want immediate emancipation and then immediate rights bestowed on all black people in the South.

ED AYERS   So can anybody just proclaim themselves an abolitionist if they want to be?

CHRISTY COLEMAN   Proclaiming oneself an abolitionist is an extraordinarily brave thing to do because there are people, North and South, who are willing to do you bodily harm for that proclamation. On one end of the spectrum you have the radical abolitionist who is advocating for full rights of African Americans. There's the other end of that spectrum that's saying we need to end slavery. We need to end what we consider to be an abomination against scripture. Either way, claiming oneself to be an abolitionist is tough. These people not only say it and believe it, but they financially support the production of pamphlets and the various speeches that people are giving around the country. Many abolitionists are also active in the formalized networks of the Underground Railroad or are themselves taking individual actions to help harbor runaways. Again, an incredibly brave thing to do.

There are a few radicals who are showing up. As a matter of fact, there is a really interesting meeting that takes place in Detroit. Detroit has a population of about 40,000 folks. There are about 1,400 free blacks in that community. It is a very prosperous African American community. There are doctors, a few teachers, ministers, and the like. They are very, very active in helping people, particularly from Kentucky and Virginia, to get up through that route and over into Windsor, Ontario. They have hosted Frederick Douglass several times. They're holding a meeting at the home of William Webb in March of this year, 1859, and they get a request from that crazy guy coming out of Kansas who wants to come and talk to this group. Now, mind you, these are very cautious folk, because they know that there are forces out there that very much want to take away what they have. But they agree to sit down and talk to John Brown at Webb's house. Folks in the city are abuzz about the fact that he's there; they remember Bleeding Kansas very well, and that makes them a little uneasy. They listen to what he has to say, and they let him know, "You're taking this ship in a direction that we're not prepared to go, so you're on your own." And they send him away.

ED AYERS   Christy, you mentioned women before. What proportion of abolitionists in the North would have been women?

CHRISTY COLEMAN   Women are very active in the abolitionist movement. It gives them the impetus to form their own women's rights movement. They're essentially being trained, if you will, in the abolitionist movement. I don't know the actual number.

JOAN WAUGH I would say about 25 percent. They are very active. The abolitionist movement is really at the end of a continuum of activism and reform, combining with the new advances in communication that make this period so remarkable for its rapid change. The Second Great Awakening, the growth of the Methodist Church and the Baptist Church, brought together the advances in communication and in printing. This social movement included African Americans, included slave and free blacks, and many women who were, in a way, through their churches, trained for positions of leadership. That's where you find these remarkable women making speeches.

WALTER JOHNSON I think it's important to think about what is the proslavery view of antislavery. There is, I think, a real fear of opponents of slavery within the United States Congress. I think there is less of a focus on the American antislavery society than our standard histories would lead us to believe. I don't have the sense that James Henry Hammond is losing a whole lot of sleep over William Lloyd Garrison. I have a sense that James Henry Hammond of South Carolina is losing a whole lot of sleep over the British. Proslavery ideologues have the idea that the British are fomenting agitation against slavery in the United States because they are interested in trying to destabilize the Southern monopoly position in the cotton market. Eighty-five percent of the world's cotton supply is produced out of the South. They believe an Atlantic-wide assault upon the institution of slavery is an effort to push them to the side so that the British can develop independent, that is, colonial, sources of cotton in India and West Africa.

GARY GALLAGHER And in Egypt.

ED AYERS Something you're emphasizing, Walter, is that this isn't just the United States thinking about itself in the 1850s. How are we connected to the world? Where else are we tied into in the 1850s? That's not what we usually see in the textbooks. Where else matters in the world to us? We say Latin America is important.

WALTER JOHNSON I think the entire geography of the world has shifted since the United States–Mexico war, not just for the defenders of slavery but also for expansionists and capitalists, and eager entrepreneurial imperialists in the United States generally. There is an emerging concern with the Pacific. What does a concern with the Pacific mean? It means there's a concern with Central America, with controlling some sort of transit across the isthmus, whether that's going to be Nicaragua or whether that's going to be Panama. When I say "map of the United States," a certain kind of picture comes to mind—the contiguous United States. But if you say "map of the United States" to James D. B. DeBow in 1859, you see a map that has the Gulf of Mexico and Cuba; it has the ninety miles between Cuba and Florida and ninety miles between Cuba and the Yucatan peninsula, and the possibility of shipping being closed out by a hostile foreign power. If shipping out of the Gulf is closed off, the entire Mississippi valley economy is closed off. Now, the emergent counter to that maritime Atlantic/Pacific/Gulf/Mississippi geography is the emergence of the railroad. There's a different economic geography emerging in the United States around the railroad.

ED AYERS   Let's talk about the railroad. I'm not sure people realize that in the twenty years between 1840 and 1860 a communications and transportation revolution occurred that's bigger than the one we've seen when the Internet took place.

GARY GALLAGHER   It's incredible. In the 1850s railroad mileage has more than quadrupled in the slaveholding states. It's more than tripled in the free states. There are more than 30,000 miles of railroad altogether now. The telegraph has gone almost everywhere. It hasn't gone across the continent yet, but it's close to going across the continent.

ED AYERS   Has it crossed the Atlantic yet?

GARY GALLAGHER   Just last year the Atlantic cable was put in place. It didn't last very long. We had an unfortunate break in the Atlantic cable, but we feel certain that will be corrected soon. It stretches from Ireland to Newfoundland. We can be in contact in minutes rather than ten days each way across the Atlantic. Space and time are shrinking in this decade. It's unbelievable. You can get to places faster. You can communicate with different places more quickly. It is reshaping the entire way that we think about economic things, political things. We have four thousand newspapers in the United States in 1859, and those can now get stories more quickly and get issues out more quickly. There's almost too much information, many people think. Things are going too quickly.

JOAN WAUGH   There's also talk of a transcontinental railroad. In the 1840s and 1850s the idea of linking the continent from east to west and from west to east has captured people's imagination. There are two engineers gripped by that dream: one named Grenville Dodge, who's looking to do surveys for completing the railroad from Iowa to the Pacific; and one named Theodore Judah, from New York, who built the first railroad in California in the late 1850s, and who wants to figure out how to get a railroad through the Sierra mountains. By 1859 they both have those surveys pretty much done.

GARY GALLAGHER   But it has become very political.

ED AYERS   What's the issue?

GARY GALLAGHER   Where is it going to be? Where is it going to start, and where's it going to end?

JOAN WAUGH   "I think it would be better through the South," say some of them.

GARY GALLAGHER   And others say, "No, it's better across a more northern route."

WALTER JOHNSON   Is it going to be Chicago, is it going to be St. Louis, or is it going to be New Orleans?

GARY GALLAGHER   Because whichever city on Walter's list gets the railroad is going to derive unbelievable economic potential.

JOAN WAUGH   Gary said something very telling in bringing up the Colorado gold rush. Just this year, 100,000 miners and other white settlers have flooded into the Colorado Territory. That 100,000 outnumbered the entire Indian population. We haven't mentioned the Indian population. In order for all this to happen, so many things had to be done, and one of them was that the Indians had to be removed so that this area could be cleared.

ED AYERS   Where are the American Indians at this point? It is now centuries after the first European contact.

WALTER JOHNSON   The 1820s and 1830s saw a process of removal from places like Alabama, Mississippi, and Louisiana. One needs to understand that the foundation of this economic boom of the 1850s is the expropriation of native land and then the application of African American labor.

ED AYERS   Where were the Indians removed to?

WALTER JOHNSON   In the first instance, people were moved mostly to Oklahoma—

GARY GALLAGHER   To Indian Territory.

WALTER JOHNSON   Yes, to the western portion of what had been Arkansas Territory. Then what you see in the 1850s, with the necessity of producing federal governance in the West so that railroad magnates' land titles can be legally vindicated, is a secondary process of Indian removal for some groups, where they're again pushed out and eventually put into reservations.

GARY GALLAGHER The government has a series of treaties with the Indians in both the southern Plains and the northern Plains. But I have good friends in the North who would say that we're placing entirely too much emphasis on what's going on with slaves and Indians. In the North, it isn't the main thing on people's minds. We're pretty sure that this census that's in the process of being finished is going to show that in the free states the population is almost 99 percent white. So there is concern in the North with issues that relate to the expansion of slavery and what they mean, for example, for white farmers in the North who might want to go west. But most people in the North don't wake up every day and have their first thought be something about the South or about slavery or about what's happening to Indians. They would be thinking about other things.

ED AYERS Like what?

GARY GALLAGHER They'd be thinking about business, economics, jobs.

ED AYERS Aren't they thinking about moving to the West?

GARY GALLAGHER Many of them are thinking of moving to the West. The West has a great allure to people because it has the commodity they need. It has land, if the Indians are removed.

JOAN WAUGH And at this time, the Plains Indians—the Cherokee, Shoshoni, the Lakota Sioux—are actually not on reservations. That is why, along with the surveys, along with plotting and getting money from entrepreneurs to fund the idea of a transcontinental railroad and securing government loans, there has to be the resolution of the Indian land issue.

GARY GALLAGHER The gold in Colorado has brought a much higher level of friction between the Plains Indians and the white miners going west.

ED AYERS What we think of now as the Old West doesn't actually exist yet, with all the cowboys and things we see?

GARY GALLAGHER That doesn't exist.

ED AYERS So what's the West like? What areas that would become states are still unorganized at this time?

GARY GALLAGHER   If you go to the western border of our new state of Minnesota and look west, you're looking at unorganized territory all the way to the Pacific Ocean. Oregon on the Pacific Ocean is a state, but there's a vast hinterland that is still Indian country. There are numerous native peoples there.

ED AYERS   So a third of the nation is still unorganized at this time, a quarter?

GARY GALLAGHER   I would say something less than a quarter, probably. But this is a big nation.

ED AYERS   While that's an exciting prospect, it's somewhat of a destabilizer to have that much area unorganized.

JOAN WAUGH   There are thousands of settlers heading out, usually from somewhere along the Missouri River. Many go to Oregon and California.

GARY GALLAGHER   As a nation, we can't quite figure out how this is going to work out in the long term. There's a significant population of Mormons in Utah. Last year Albert Sydney Johnston commanded a military expedition into Utah. Many in the country are afraid the Mormons don't really fit in.

JOAN WAUGH   There seem to be more of them every year.

GARY GALLAGHER   So we sent the United States Army to Utah in 1858, and things seem quiet there right now.

ED AYERS   So why are they in Utah?

GARY GALLAGHER   They're in Utah because they have been driven out of successive other places they've lived in the United States. Many of their neighbors would say that they were driven out because they're odd. I suspect the Mormons would have a different explanation for that. There's been a great deal of violence against Mormon leaders. Their most important leader, Joseph Smith, was killed. They have a new principal leader now that they're out west, a man named Brigham Young. But they are a piece of a picture in our western lands that's really different from any other picture.

ED AYERS   So everything seems to be in flux. Something we've not talked about very much is Northern cities and industrial growth. When we think of the United States at this period, we think about industrialization. Christy said we have all these Irish and Germans flooding into cities as other people are flooding out to new lands of the West. What are the major cities of the North, and how are they changing? What does industry look like?

GARY GALLAGHER   New York is our largest city. Brooklyn is a very large city. New York is right at about a million people. Philadelphia is still a great city. But as Joan mentioned, we have great river cities in the West. St. Louis is a great city; Cincinnati is a great city.

ED AYERS   These are all new cities?

GARY GALLAGHER   Yes, those western ones are newer.

WALTER JOHNSON   I think it may be the case that in our standard history we have overemphasized the industrial transformation of the North. These cities are still largely mercantile cities in the late 1850s. They are largely importing, buying, and selling. There is an emergent industrial or manufacturing sector, and it is more prominent in the North than it is in the South. But really the manufacturing in the world is occurring in Great Britain.

ED AYERS   What's manufacturing like in the 1850s?

WALTER JOHNSON   Manufacturing in the 1850s is largely the manufacturing of low-quality goods used to clothe slaves—shoes and low-quality clothes.

ED AYERS   We're not good enough to make the good stuff, right? We have to import that?

WALTER JOHNSON   That's a really important point because it gestures to the fact that our traditional separation of the industrial North and slaveholding South covers over a series of much more complex interchanges, particularly economic interchanges.

GARY GALLAGHER   The census is going to deal with this, of course. I think it's going to tell us what the most powerful parts of the manufacturing sector are. Flour and meal are going to be the most important part of the manufacturing sector by a very wide margin. Cotton goods will come second. Finished lumber will come third. And shoes, as Walter mentioned, will be fourth. Various kinds of clothing will be fifth. Nowhere on that list is iron production. Nowhere on that list is rail production of any kind. As Walter said, it is a different kind of manufacturing picture than people might see down the road a ways.

There are about a million men engaged in manufacturing jobs. That's what the census is going to show us. There are more than a quarter of a million women engaged in the manufacturing sector.

One out of five manufacturing jobs in the United States is held by a woman. Many of them are in our northeastern textile industry, which is a powerful part of our economic engine.

Again, picking up on what Walter said, there are cities in the South that look very much like cities in the North. Richmond, Virginia, is a perfect example. Some of the largest flour mills in the world are in Richmond, Virginia.

JOAN WAUGH   I just have one word for this panel. That's "tariff." If your manufacturing isn't that important, why is the tariff so important? The debate over the tariff, the tax on imported goods—its reason for existence is to strengthen American manufacturers. Manufacturing is growing, and in fact as small as the cities are at this time, relative to what they would be later, the fact is that the degree of change in urbanization was higher in the 1840s and '50s than it would be at any other time. Huge markets are being created that have to be serviced. This is a challenge, and businesses are rising to that challenge.

ED AYERS   So is the tariff a leading political issue?

WALTER JOHNSON   The tariff is a huge issue. It's not necessarily indicative of the strength of the manufacturing sector, but it's indicative of some people's vision that there needs to be a stronger manufacturing sector. To come back to the South, almost every tract in Southern political economy that I've read from 1837 to 1859 returns to a single statistic, which is that the South accounts for two-thirds of the nation's exports and consumes only one-fifth of its imported goods. Defenders of slavery and proslavery political economists view the increment between those two as the increment that is being skimmed off by the Northern mercantile commercial sector and by the federal government. These Southerners are writing about the tariff and also the various sorts of navigation acts, the development of ports, and subsidies to Massachusetts cod fishermen. They're absolutely obsessed with subsidies to Massachusetts cod fishermen. All of these things have led to the economic overdevelopment of the North and the dispossession of the rights of those who, they believe, produce the greatest wealth in the world. What they don't mention, of course, is the fundamental dispossession—that they are not the ones who are producing the cotton that is running the global economy. It's their slaves. There's a hole in the middle of that argument, but this is an argument which comes up again and again.

GARY GALLAGHER   But the South has a favorable tariff now. They got a tariff in 1857 that drops the rates significantly, to the degree that President Buchanan's administration thinks that it's not an issue now, or at least shouldn't be the hot issue that it was. The rate has come down to about 20 percent. That is a significant concession.

ED AYERS   They think maybe they're making progress on this tariff?

GARY GALLAGHER   That maybe they're making progress.

ED AYERS   It's not building up in the 1850s because it's been a topic for twenty-five years. We have talked about the panorama of American population. Let's talk about the African Americans who are not enslaved. Where do they live and how many of them are there?

CHRISTY COLEMAN   We were estimating that there are roughly four million enslaved people. The free black population in the South is relatively low, about 3 to 4 percent are free people. They're living in the same places that enslaved people are. Being a free black person doesn't mean that you have all of the rights and abilities. In fact, the court has ruled several times that you don't have any rights at all; and the ruling covered not only African Americans but Native Americans, people of mixed race, and so on.

GARY GALLAGHER   And women.

CHRISTY COLEMAN   Yes, women too. Here in Richmond there is a relatively vibrant free black population. They're working down at Tredegar Iron Works, they're working in the warehouses, and they're working on farms. Some of them are involved in skilled trades. Some are landholders, the so-called elite free blacks. They tend to be the barbers and preachers and come from similar walks of life. Their lifestyle is very precarious, especially if they're in the Southern portions of the nation, because unless someone white is willing to verify your freedom in a court, a catcher or someone who has a beef with you can challenge you at any time. The so-called manumission or free papers or certificates of freedom are not really registered. Free blacks are living outside the society but being affected by it.

GARY GALLAGHER   They're located primarily in an arc from Rhode Island, swinging around the coast, down to below Philadelphia. New Jersey has more free black people than any other Northern state. About 3 percent of New Jersey's population is free black.

CHRISTY COLEMAN   Baltimore's free black population is pretty large as well.

ED AYERS   But there's not really a safe place to go if you're a free black person, right?

JOAN WAUGH   Canada.

WALTER JOHNSON   Or Mexico.

GARY GALLAGHER   Or Nicaragua, if William Walker doesn't have his way.

WALTER JOHNSON   The other thing to say about the late 1850s, in relationship to free people of color, is there are active, although largely unsuccessful, efforts to re-enslave free people of color in a lot of Southern states. A re-enslavement law is passed in Louisiana in 1859 that allows free people voluntarily to enslave themselves. It's not taken up by a whole lot of people. I think that those laws reach the point where proslavery collapses under the weight of its own absurdity. The laws are, however, indicative of a larger social and political effort to get rid of free people of color in the South, to render them illegal because they're contradictory.

CHRISTY COLEMAN   For proslavery arguments, the fact is there are a lot of people who strongly believe that the perfect state for the black person is enslavement, that this is a population that needs to be controlled, and that God has ordained that white people control them. The best thing that ever happened to Africans, white Southerners argue, is that they got Christianized and put into slavery to control them.

GARY GALLAGHER   That issue has split major churches. Both the Baptists and Methodists have formally split. They can't agree on how to handle slavery.

JOAN WAUGH   Part of the Northern Methodist and the Northern Baptist churches—may I inject a glimmer of hope in this otherwise grim story?—founded colleges in Ohio, Lane and Oberlin, that African American students could attend. There were other states, such as Massachusetts, which opened up their schools to African American students. But it's this religious connection with evangelical religion and abolitionism that really provided the most welcoming part of the equation for free blacks.

GARY GALLAGHER   Some of the proslavery ideologues carry the argument beyond color. George Fitzhugh argues that many white people should be enslaved too. There are people who shouldn't be slaves, and there are people who should be slaves. His was an extreme case, but the argument, carried to its logical extension, takes you there, and that's where he is willing to go.

ED AYERS   I have to admit, I'm really uncomfortable in this conversation because it sounds like the country is in really precarious shape here in 1859.

CHRISTY COLEMAN   We talk about all these things that are going on, yet people are still going to concerts, they're still going out and buying all this wonderful mass-produced music. They're going to bandstands and listening to these brass bands. It's the latest wave. Ninety-nine percent of white Northerners don't know a thing about black people and couldn't care less about black people in some cases. They're going to shows that Stephen Foster and others are putting on, and they're watching these entertaining depictions of people bouncing around, doing Jim Crow.

ED AYERS   Minstrel shows, the most popular entertainment in the country.

CHRISTY COLEMAN   The most popular entertainment in the country. You've got Northerners whistling "Dixie" and thinking it's the best song. It came out of the tradition of minstrel shows. People are basically living their lives. It's these little thorny things that keep popping up. Most people don't wake up in the morning in 1859 and say, "My God, the nation is on the precipice."

ED AYERS   It's the eve of the Civil War. They don't know it.

GARY GALLAGHER   They don't get up and say, "Isn't it great living in the antebellum years?" They don't know they're living in the antebellum years.

JOAN WAUGH   I would suggest there is unease. While you can live life and enjoy things around you, you are also reading newspaper accounts about the debates in Congress, even the canings in Congress. There is a political polarization that's going on in this country, and there's a political mobilization.

ED AYERS   As you can see, there are many unresolved dramas as we look at this panorama of the United States in 1859.

View of the Tredegar Iron Works, with footbridge to Neilson's Island, Richmond, Virginia; photograph by Alexander Gardner. (Library of Congress, Prints and Photographs Division)

2 THE FUTURE OF VIRGINIA AND THE SOUTH

Presenters were Charles Dew, Robert Kenzer, Gregg Kimball, and Lauranett Lee, with Edward L. Ayers moderating.

ED AYERS We have talked about the state of the United States in 1859. Where does the South fit in those trends? Is the South outside of those trends, or is it a part of them?

CHARLES DEW I think the South is doing quite well, but it depends on who you are in the South as to how well you are doing. The percentage of Southern families who own slaves, roughly 25 percent, are doing extremely well. I think the rocketing slave prices in the 1850s were a phenomenon. Southerners are drawing a good deal of comfort from that in thinking about the future. I think they see a very prosperous future, if they can keep the political turmoil from interrupting their enterprises, particularly agriculture. In Richmond, there is real prosperity. Tredegar Iron Works is doing well. It's expanding, adding workers, adding manufacturing operations. Richmond is a flour-milling boomtown. The biggest export of flour from anywhere in the country is coming right from the James River in Richmond, down to Norfolk and then throughout the world. The Shenandoah Valley is feeding that industry with grain. I think you've got a pretty good sense of prosperity in Virginia, particularly since the 1857 depression that hit everywhere else didn't affect the South as it did a lot of the country.

ED AYERS How long did that depression last?

BOB KENZER It was about a year. It was somewhat related to trends that were already underway in the United States, but the Crimean War stimulated farmers, particularly Northern farmers, to grow a lot more grain. When that war ended, that really did hurt the North more than the South. I think that Charles is right; Richmond is doing well. Agricultural Virginia, rural Virginia, isn't doing quite as well. The population of Virginia has grown in this decade by about 12 percent, whereas in the United States as a whole it has grown by 36 percent. By many agricultural measurements—the number of farms, for example—Virginia has grown at half the rate of the rest of the country. In improved acreage, it has grown at only one-fourth the national rate. So I think there are some problems. The tobacco sector has kept pace and is a leading area of growth in this period. But there are long-term problems in Virginia. There are some transformations taking place in the economy. But Virginia is a net exporter of people—African Americans, because of the moving slave trade, and whites as well. To me the person who most embodies this is Cyrus McCormick, the inventor of the reaper. McCormick was born on February 15, 1809, three days after Abraham Lincoln was born. We're not celebrating his birthday in 2009, as I think we should. Significantly, this great inventor, this great Southerner from Rockbridge County, moves to Chicago. A lot of native Virginians, white Virginians, have to make very difficult choices, particularly those from the agricultural sector.

GREGG KIMBALL   In generalizing about Virginia, we have to remember that Virginia is Wheeling as well as Richmond. There's an Appalachian region that in many ways embodies the regional diversity of the entire South. There isn't a South that's coherent economically, in my view. Virginia's really nothing like Louisiana, although they're very connected in some ways.

ED AYERS   Virginia would be one of the largest states, wouldn't it, if it includes what will become West Virginia?

GREGG KIMBALL   Exactly.

LAURANETT LEE   Let me add that free blacks are experiencing a very difficult time. There are instances where people are being kidnapped and sold into slavery. Even those blacks who become freed are forced to leave the state because of a law that has been put into place. One man, upon being forced to leave, remarked, "Virginia, with all thy faults, I love thee still." Virginia is home to a lot of people, but they are forced to leave family and everything they know to go to territories that they have no knowledge about. A painting by Lefevre Cranstone, an English artist who traveled the countryside of southeast America, captures an image of what is possibly a free black woman in southwest Virginia. We know that many free blacks rely on patronage ties to protect them, but sometimes those patronage ties are not enough.

ED AYERS   This sounds like a mixed bag. Virginia is changing a lot. Charles mentioned something that's surprising to a lot of people. What is the largest crop in Virginia in 1859?

BOB KENZER   With no question, it would be the wheat crop. The wheat crop is expanding, but it is expanding at a much slower rate than it is nationally as Kansas and new states in the Midwest are opening up. The advantages of growing wheat are not what they were before. Virginia has tried to recover for many years by shifting to grains. If anything is an emerging crop, it is a new bright leaf tobacco planted south of Richmond all the way to the North Carolina border. Virginia and North Carolina are experiencing a new cash crop.

ED AYERS   I thought tobacco was back in the seventeenth century?

BOB KENZER   It's a new kind of tobacco, replacing the burley tobacco that had been grown. That tobacco had a poor yield in the Tidewater area. So this is a new era of tobacco growth. That is the one emerging sector where surely Virginia is holding its own. The expectation would be that in the next number of decades that might become a dominant crop to help sustain the loss of population, particularly in those counties south and west of Richmond.

ED AYERS   So grain is not as big as in the Midwest?

BOB KENZER   Right.

ED AYERS   But Charles was talking about these big mills. If you take the Canal Walk today, you're basically walking underneath mills. Explain how this works. You said this wheat is coming from the Shenandoah Valley, but is most of the state growing wheat?

CHARLES DEW   Corn is a major crop; we all know about Virginia hams. There is a thriving corn and hog complex in the Commonwealth. Truck farming is beginning to develop around major cities. I think Hanover tomatoes are well known in this area today. There is a much more diversified agricultural picture in Virginia. You couldn't grow cotton in Virginia. There weren't enough frost-free days. So

Virginia lost out on cotton. If you are farming in Virginia, you are looking for alternatives. Grains certainly are a major part of it. Interestingly enough, one of the reasons McCormick heads out to the Midwest is the farmers in the valley said that it's too rocky and rolling and hilly here. These reapers don't do us much good. So the slaves are out using scythes and doing it the old-fashioned way.

ED AYERS   And where do they ship it?

CHARLES DEW   All over the world.

GREGG KIMBALL   Australia.

CHARLES DEW   Latin America. There is a huge trade to Latin America out of the Richmond flour industry.

ED AYERS   It strikes me that this story of Richmond and its ties to the international economy is one that a lot of people don't know. Richmond is a vital node for the United States as a whole.

GREGG KIMBALL   I think of Richmond and central Virginia as the southernmost tier of a mid-Atlantic system. It has the best-developed railroad networks that connect up to places like Washington and Baltimore. It's less connected commercially in most ways to the rest of the South than it is to New York, which is a real irony. If you're a merchant in Richmond and you want goods, you go to New York. Now, the exceptions to that are the railroad industry, where a lot of goods are being sold to Southern railroads, and, of course, the slave trade.

CHARLES DEW   Don't forget coal. The coal mines around Richmond are the largest in the East. They are funneling enormous amounts of coal out of the state and up the Atlantic seaboard.

ED AYERS   So Virginia in 1859 looks nothing like we think it did. When people picture "the South" on the eve of the Civil War, Virginia doesn't fit that?

BOB KENZER   Well, the problem, I think, is just the way you express it, "the South." The South has so many different components, whether we're talking about Appalachia, Mississippi, Virginia, Maryland, whatever. I think if there's one stereotype we have, and as people probably had in 1859, it is that there's a united South, ideologically, economically, or demographically. That's simply not the case. Diversity is as much the case in the South as in the North.

ED AYERS   We should remember that the South is the size of continental Europe. But people do not picture what we now think of as the map of the South—the boundaries are not clear at all. Presenters have talked about all the way down to Cuba and Mexico, and how far west does the South go?

LAURANETT LEE We might mention also, when we think about crops, that the enslaved people of the area are considered a crop because Virginia is very much involved in the slave trade, particularly the internal trade. The domestic slave trade had become a major economic enterprise by 1815. Enslaved people are shackled and marched down through various parts of Virginia. I think about the Alexandria slave pens, Franklin & Armfield in particular. There are a multitude of slave-trading businesses in Richmond itself. Auction houses, hotels, slave stores that cater to the slave trade. It is much bigger than we could imagine.

ED AYERS Describe what the slave trade would have looked like here.

CHARLES DEW This image is what popped into my mind first: In a page from the 1858 Richmond Business Directory we can get a sense of just how average and ordinary slave trading is in the 1850s. There are some lawyers in here and some people who auction real estate and so on. If you look at the bottom third of the page you see "Hector Davis, Auctioneer and Commission Merchant for the sale of Negroes." It was as normal as selling corn or salt or sugar or anything. "Franklin Street, Richmond, Sells Negroes both publicly and privately and pledges his best efforts to obtain the highest market prices." This is a relatively standard pitch. "He has a safe and commodious jail where he boards all Negroes intended for his sales at 30 cents a day." Here's a prosperous businessman. If you look at the amount of business he is doing, it's staggering. Another image will certainly confirm what Lauranett was saying about how big this trade was. Hector Davis's account books are in the Chicago Historical Society. I was up there this past summer, and I realized that there was a weekly sales figure. Since you have that, you can do a monthly and then a yearly. And these are his figures: in 1858 one Richmond auction house did $1,773,000-plus in slave sales.

ED AYERS How much would that be in 2009?

CHARLES DEW You'd multiply that at least by a factor of 20 to get into contemporary purchasing power. If you look at 1859, at sort of the peak of the antebellum slave market, you see the sum of $2,671,000.

This is really an extraordinary business. And it's worked at a highly developed level, using the telegraph, using the railroads, using every modern convenience, the transportation and communication revolutions that are taking place. The slave trade is plugged into all of them. Hector Davis's is one of four major auction houses in Richmond, so I think you could probably take his figures and multiply them by four, five, or six to get a sense of how big this is for Richmond as a commercial center.

BOB KENZER   How would the profits of slave trading compare to, say, Tredegar Iron Works at this time?

CHARLES DEW   Nowhere near the profit level of the slave trade business. And I have one last image on this topic. The slave auction houses in Richmond put out price lists. Another image is a price list of one of the Richmond firms, a firm by the name of Betts & Gregory. It's a printed form where you can fill in the figures. There are categories, and then the price range is there, and generally a little note at the bottom. That first line of handwritten text says, "Good young woman and first child, $1300–1450." I'm sure that people can figure that one out pretty quickly: here's a woman who has proved that she can have children, and that's a commodity in the market. It's a business that's hugely important. Its human dimensions are almost impossible to fathom. But it is very much a part of Richmond's history, and Virginia's. Virginia is a major exporting state when it comes to slaves.

LAURANETT LEE   When we see these numbers, it really does put things in perspective. Maria Perkins, an enslaved woman from Charlottesville, wrote to her husband, who was in Staunton, begging him to raise the money to buy her and her son before they were sold. We come across these letters, and it puts a human perspective on this huge slave-trading business.

GREGG KIMBALL   There are a number of accounts similar to that of a young New York clerk who comes to Richmond to work in a dry goods store who inevitably stumbles into one of these slave sales. He's appalled to see someone examine the slave's teeth and his body, but at the same time, he goes on with his life. He writes of his disgust, but it really doesn't change anything for him.

ED AYERS   Is there a stigma associated with being involved in this business?

GREGG KIMBALL We know there were at least two city council members in Richmond who were slave traders. I think one of the enduring myths about the slave trade is that it carried a social stigma. I don't believe that.

ED AYERS If contemporary visitors to Richmond were to go see where slave trading took place, where is that, and what would it look like today?

LAURANETT LEE Shockoe Bottom. The Capitol Square is very near. You can walk to Shockoe Bottom from there. In 1858 the Virginia Washington Equestrian Monument was unveiled. It's a beautiful monument that we are able to see now. African Americans were not allowed on Capitol Square, yet those who attended this unveiling—those whites—were able to walk or ride to Shockoe Bottom to participate in slave trading. We get a sense of the separate spheres on Capitol Square and how close in proximity they are.

GREGG KIMBALL It is ubiquitous. We know, for instance, that there are sales held in the St. Charles Hotel, which is a very fine establishment in Shockoe Bottom. And it's worth noting, too, that the city is currently [in 2009] doing excavation on Robert Lumpkin's slave jail, which is where Anthony Burns was imprisoned before he was resold into slavery.

LAURANETT LEE It was Anthony Burns who actually wrote later that he saw through a peephole while he was imprisoned there how the women and girls were examined. It's something that shocks our sensibilities to this day. Another painting by Lefevre Cranstone provides a relatively sanitized version of the interior of an auction house. We know that it is a dirty place. It is a place where you would not find Southern ladies. Central in this image are black women and children on the stand. Generally slaveholders try to keep young girls with older women in the sale. Boys are sold at a younger age than girls, and they are moved around more frequently. We see the disruption of African American families within spaces like this.

ED AYERS So how many such places would there be in Richmond? Charles has talked about the large ones, but are there small businesspeople who are slave traders?

CHARLES DEW Yes, there are dozens of traders. There are probably half a dozen major auction houses.

LAURANETT LEE   And at least nineteen auctioneers. Keep in mind, also, that there are stores that cater to slave traders. Before enslaved people are put up on the auction block, they are dressed to appear better looking and more healthy than they are so that they will command a higher sale price. These stores proliferate in this area. The adaptation of slavery to hiring is going on at the same time. Many of these same traders are hiring slaves yearly. It's clearly a reflection of adjusting to an industrial environment where you don't know how many workers you're going to need.

ED AYERS   Explain what you mean by "hiring."

GREGG KIMBALL   There is a hiring season, usually around the end of the year. Just as slaves are brought to market, they are brought in during these hiring seasons, and they are hired by a tobacco manufacturer, for instance, for a period of time—a year is typical. It's also happening in the countryside. It's not just an urban phenomenon. It gives elasticity to the labor market, essentially. It's a way that slavery is adapting to this industrial environment.

ED AYERS   So a lot of non-slaveholders, in other words, can rent the labor of the slaves.

GREGG KIMBALL   That's absolutely right.

ED AYERS   Does that help smooth over some of these tensions between slaveholders and non-slaveholders?

CHARLES DEW   I happen to think it does. The hiring market is a very, very important part of the Virginia economy. Richmond's industry really depends on it. The tobacco factories hire hundreds of slaves. Tredegar hires slaves every year. The tobacco manufacturers don't have lodging for their workers; rather, they give a small amount of money to the hired slaves and send them out in the city to find a place to board. From a slave's perspective, that's not necessarily a bad thing. You're getting some room to maneuver. Also, almost all industrial slaves work on a task basis. Once they meet their task, they begin earning money for themselves.

ED AYERS   Once they process a certain amount of tobacco, they are done for the day?

CHARLES DEW   Exactly.

ED AYERS   Then they can earn more money. What would be the incentive of earning money if you're an enslaved person?

CHARLES DEW   Because it's money you control, and you can buy whatever you wish with it. The masters are very, very smart. They know that if they can motivate the slave to some extent to work in the master's interest, it is much better than using coercion. Coercion is the cement that holds everything together, but you can't whip a skilled slave and expect that slave to do the work you want him or her to do.

GREGG KIMBALL   In terms of the dynamic with white working people, there's another problem here, though, and that is at Tredegar Iron Works. In 1847 there's a strike of the white workers because Joseph Reed Anderson, the ironmaster, decides he wants them to train enslaved workers in the rolling mills. This is highly skilled work, done mostly by British workers. The Tredegar name comes from Wales. He's asking these workers to help train people who they think are beneath them socially and in every other way. In every other place in the world, these workers would have had the right to choose their helpers.

ED AYERS   Often their sons.

GREGG KIMBALL   That's right. It's a double slap in the face. They walk out of the mill. That kind of labor conflict is occurring on a national scale. It's also happening in Richmond.

ED AYERS   Christy Coleman talked about conflict between the Irish and African Americans. Would that have happened here in Richmond?

GREGG KIMBALL   Yes. The typographical union had a strike because of the way that a certain newspaper decided to use slave workers. It's a little more muted because I think masters exert a lot of control, but I think the use of slaves is definitely a factor.

ED AYERS   How many Irish people and other immigrants are here in Richmond, Gregg?

GREGG KIMBALL   About 13 percent of Richmond's population is foreign born.

ED AYERS   And how does that compare with other cities in the South?

GREGG KIMBALL   There are some cities in the South, like Memphis, that have very high numbers of immigrants. And New Orleans. It's not as high as in those cities, but it's still substantial. And think about this: about one in five white people are foreign born.

ED AYERS   It sounds like if you were visiting Richmond, you'd see a place that is changing pretty rapidly. This population of immigrants has been here in the last fifteen years—really the last ten years.

GREGG KIMBALL The vast majority of them. There are some that came earlier, but most of them have come since 1840, 1845.

ED AYERS So you see new crops emerging, ships going down the James River with wheat for Australia, and the very large trade in slavery. All these things are happening at the same time. Railroads are coming into the city. It is hard to know what the future of the South will be. Is Richmond what the South looks like?

CHARLES DEW Good question. I think one of the things Richmond shows is how adaptable slavery is to changing economic circumstances. You can't look at the city in 1859 and not recognize the vital role that slavery is playing and the way in which those who want to use slave labor are finding ways to do so. In industrial settings, again, you use the task system so that the slave has some interest in doing this work.

GREGG KIMBALL There are some natural advantages—coal and other resources—that give Richmond and Virginia a leg up industrially. I don't think Mississippi is going to look like Virginia any time soon. But perhaps in North Carolina, perhaps the Upper South, you might see a transformation eventually.

LAURANETT LEE You also begin to see insurance policies taken out on enslaved workers, particularly in the factories. The work that they do, particularly in the factories, is dangerous. Oftentimes, they'll lose a limb, arm, finger, hand. Slave owners want to protect their property. Legislators debate the feasibility of having these insurance policies, and Richmond legislators do see it as something important.

ED AYERS It sounds to me as if slavery is a big business. It's banking, insurance, trade, and clothing. I read a remarkable fact that the enslaved population of the South as property is worth more than all the railroads and factories of the United States combined in 1859.

LAURANETT LEE Enslaved women are central to this because not only can they work, they can reproduce.

ED AYERS Let's talk about Virginia's role in the South. Is Virginia really the South?

BOB KENZER I recently looked at Virginia's political state and its share of the United States House of Representatives. The state is ex-

periencing an amazing decline. In 1800, 13 percent of the members of
the House of Representatives were from Virginia. If you will, it was
like California today. By 1860 it would be under 4.5 percent. It goes
from its height in 1810, when there were twenty-two congressmen
from the state, to eleven. Virginia is losing political power. It is losing
it to other Southern states, but it is losing it to the growing population
of the North even more rapidly.

We think of those initial presidents from Virginia, and it's under-
standable why so many of the early presidents were from Virginia.
Virginia was a dominant political power. That power is being lost over
time. That is not to say that the political figures of the 1850s are not
illustrious, but they simply don't have the national stage that they had
before.

ED AYERS   Does Virginia resent other Southern states for taking its
political power and national leadership?

BOB KENZER   Virginia still has more representation than most other
Southern states. It's not as if they've fallen behind other states like
Georgia. What's happened is that the South as a whole is losing in the
House, at least; and the South is losing in the Senate now with the five
new free states. Virginia is part of a larger pattern, but in some ways,
because it was so powerful early on, its loss, relatively speaking, is
more keenly felt. Georgia hasn't lost anything because it was never at
that level. I think Virginians feel a sense of loss of influence and power
in the government.

GREGG KIMBALL   I also have a sense that the politicians of the day are
simply not up to the task. We're talking about people whose reference
point is Washington and Jefferson. There's a comment by a young
man who's a merchant, talking about the American Party, the anti-
immigrant party at the time, and the Democrats. He describes them
as a party of intolerance on one side and one with threadbare arguments on the other. He goes to these political rallies and just can't get
fired up because he doesn't see people who really have the stature, the
ability, the drive.

ED AYERS   It's a little poignant to be putting up that huge statue on
Capitol Square of George Washington and Patrick Henry—

GREGG KIMBALL   Memorialization is going crazy across the state and
in Richmond. They're honoring their dead heroes of the Revolution,

and in a way, I think, reinforcing both their Virginianess and their Americaness, but grappling with those concepts.

ED AYERS Does the rest of the South look to Virginia as a leader?

CHARLES DEW I think the answer is yes. Virginia is still the preeminent slave state. There are more slaves in Virginia than anywhere else.

ED AYERS How many?

BOB KENZER 490,000.

CHARLES DEW Virginia is the preeminent Southern state, and Virginia's decision about what to do should a crisis come is critical.

BOB KENZER But there is an increasing loss, a relative loss, of power from the Upper South to the Lower South because of the shift in wealth. I think the way you just put it is quite accurate. If a crisis were to come, Virginia would face a very difficult question because increasingly, like Maryland, like Delaware, it is being pulled northward.

ED AYERS We hear that Virginia, Richmond in particular, is the center of the domestic slave trade. Do we have a sense of how many enslaved people would be sold out of Richmond on an annual basis, say, in 1859?

CHARLES DEW In the ads in the papers, which are running daily, Hector Davis advertises that he will sell fifty a day; Dickinson & Hill, fifty a day; Davis, Deupree & Co., thirty a day; Pulliam, twenty-five a day; Betts & Gregory, twenty. And these are just the ones that have standard ads running. You multiply that by about 352 because I don't think they sell on Sunday. But it's a large figure.

ED AYERS So thousands. And they're being brought from all over the state to Richmond, right?

CHARLES DEW Absolutely.

ED AYERS Ironically, these new railroads are facilitating that. So as the state becomes more modern, it also uses that modernity to accelerate slavery. But if there are so many slaves being sold here, how does Virginia still have the most slaves in 1860 of any Southern state?

CHARLES DEW Because the slave population and the free population, we know from the census, increase at just about the same rate every ten years. The white population increases 26–27 percent every ten years; the slave population, 24–25 percent, something like that. You've got this phenomenon of the only slave system we've ever known anywhere in the world where the system sustains itself by natural increase.

LAURANETT LEE In fact many slave owners encourage enslaved women to have children. Thomas Jefferson, for example, would give an extra peck of corn or an extra blanket, something like that. We also realize that there are freed people who choose to re-enslave themselves. There are petitions asking to be re-enslaved so that they can stay.

ED AYERS Why do they do that, Lauranett? To stay with their families?

LAURANETT LEE Well, supposedly. But also because Virginia was home and all that home means, such as family and familiarity. With that comes a relative freedom from the unfamiliar.

GREGG KIMBALL But there are also many free African Americans who are leaving. They're going to Liberia. They're going to places like Philadelphia, Detroit. If you look at the minutes of First African Baptist Church, every session there's a list of people who are asking for their letters to go to a new church in a new location.

ED AYERS Let's talk about the church. We have the largest black church in America, I believe, the First African Baptist Church here in Richmond. So black people and white people have the same religion?

GREGG KIMBALL They share the Baptist and Methodist religions, certainly. In the case of the church you mentioned, the white and black congregations separate in 1841; they had previously been together although in segregated seating. And so you had the creation of this incredibly large church. In fact, about a fifth of the total black population is going to this one church. The president of the University of Richmond, Robert Ryland, was the minister because they were not allowed to have a black minister.

ED AYERS So the churches are both segregated and integrated.

GREGG KIMBALL In the countryside, I think you're going to see integrated churches; whereas in the cities, you start to see a development of African churches.

CHARLES DEW Slaves sit toward the rear or in a balcony in an average church, but many churches are integrated. Of course, rural slaves hold their own prayer meetings. We know that they hear a much different gospel there than they hear from white preachers. White preachers preach the same sermon over and over again, "Servants, obey your masters." And the slaves take that in one ear, and it goes out the other. Then they have their own prayer meetings, and their own vibrant religious culture develops in a much different context than the whites realize. Whites are leery of this. They worry about these clandestine meetings.

ED AYERS   Do whites who go to church feel guilty about slavery?

GREGG KIMBALL   There may be some who see it as a necessary evil, shall we say. There are people like John Hartwell Cocke, who trained his slaves to be emancipated and then sent them to Liberia. It's certainly true that you have women's rights activists and abolitionists here. But you have the other classic kinds of reforms. You have temperance. The Sons of Temperance are here. You have religious reform ideas. And there are people like Cocke who are far from the vanguard. But he's limited in what he can do.

ED AYERS   He led a campaign against tobacco.

GREGG KIMBALL   He did. But he's limited in how he can do these things.

CHARLES DEW   Absolutely. And I think the answer to your guilt question is no. I think the incidence of white guilt among Southerners and slave owners is minuscule. I think if you felt that way, you tended to leave. If you were James G. Birney, you left and became an abolitionist and a leader of the Liberty Party. As has been mentioned, whites think they are doing Africans a favor. They argue that slavery is a form of uplift, that we have saved the barbaric African from heathenism and all the other things that happened on the so-called Dark Continent. I've often thought of my own experience growing up in the South when the South was segregated. Here you were looking at something that was inherently evil every day and not seeing it. I think that many, many white Southerners of 1859 do exactly the same thing.

GREGG KIMBALL   There's a wonderful account of Fredrika Bremer, a Swedish reformer, visiting Richmond. She goes to the First African Baptist Church, and it's being used for a Fourth of July celebration because it is the largest venue in the city. Democratic and Whig conventions met there. It is used by other groups as the main meeting house. She just couldn't get her head around this. They're talking about liberty and freedom, and here they are. Don't they understand that this is a total contradiction? But no, they don't. People have an enormous capacity to ignore things that are inconvenient to them.

BOB KENZER   I think that we also have to understand that only about one in four or five Virginians owns slaves. Although they're part of that slave-owning culture, and in fact they might rent slaves, the vast majority of people don't have ownership. So they're probably not thinking the ways those who own them do. Some Virginians, of course, live in the western part of the state where there are virtually no slaves at all.

ED AYERS   But it's important to know that slavery is growing very rapidly in parts that we now think of as Appalachia. So in Bristol, Abingdon, those areas, slavery is actually getting stronger, not fading away.

BOB KENZER   I'm talking farther west.

LAURANETT LEE   And then there's the colonization movement. There are some prominent people who believe very strongly that rather than have enslaved people here, we should educate them and send them out of Virginia. Women, particularly Mary Custis, believed that if enslaved people could be educated, they would do well. She herself educated the slaves on her plantation.

ED AYERS   That became illegal later, right?

LAURANETT LEE   Yes, very much so. You have Dangerfield Newby. His father was a white slave owner, and his mother enslaved. His father freed him and all the siblings, and they moved. Dangerfield Newby tried to free his family. His wife, Harriet, lived in Prince William County, and she wrote three letters to him. In one of Harriet's letters to Dangerfield she spoke about their young daughter, Lucy, who was just beginning to crawl. And she asked that Dangerfield come to see them, money or no money. And then in another letter she asked him to buy them because the slave master was going to sell them. Dangerfield Newby raised $741.55 toward the $1,000 that the slave master wanted. It was not enough, and Harriet and the son were sold.

ED AYERS   Sometimes we find enslaved people using new technology to escape. Somebody tell the story of Henry "Box" Brown.

GREGG KIMBALL   Brown was an enslaved tobacco factory worker. His wife was owned by another master. He made extensive attempts to purchase his family and children. But in the end, they were sold south. He resolved to get himself out of the city, and with the assistance of a white shoemaker, he boxed himself into a box and was put on the railroad. It gives us an education in infrastructure, too, because he was, of course, moved many times. You forget you had to get on a steamboat to get from the RF&P Railroad to a connection in

Washington and several other connections where he was turned up-side down. This box had little holes he had drilled to breathe through. It was quite an ordeal. He made it to Philadelphia, and as had been planned, a group of abolitionists unboxed him. He went on to be a very well-known abolitionist speaker. He developed a panorama show called "The Mirror of Slavery" to tell the story. He went to England. It is a fascinating story about how technology allowed him to escape.

ED AYERS   The title of this session has the whole South in it. We've dwelled on Virginia, which is only fitting given this is the Virginia sesquicentennial. But let's think about this area that's the size of continental Europe. Portray for me what different parts of the South would look like in the late 1850s. What's happening elsewhere in the South?

BOB KENZER   One way of looking at the difference is the share of population that's African American. In Louisiana, in South Carolina, we're talking about a black majority population. Along the Mississippi Delta, in certain areas, about 80 percent of the population is African American and overwhelmingly enslaved. The scale of slave owning in these areas in contrast to Virginia is staggering. We're talking about very large plantations, some with over a thousand slaves who virtually never see their masters. They have overseers. Their daily lives would be different, too, because of the difference in crops. Quite simply, growing grains versus growing tobacco versus growing cotton, seasonally things are very different. It's still an agricultural lifestyle, overwhelmingly, but the patterns are different. You're dependent on different markets over the whole world. If you're a cotton grower, increasingly, you might be influenced by how much cotton is being grown in Egypt. If you're a grain grower, you're influenced by what's going on in the war in the Crimea.

There's tremendous variation in the South, and a lot of that variation has to do with crops, but it also has to do with the percentage of the population that's enslaved, and the percentage of whites who own slaves. Those societies, as I was saying earlier, are extremely different. When we get into the Southwest and Texas, you've got mixtures of the population with the German population; same thing throughout Missouri, for example in the St. Louis area. Again the term "the South" is almost a meaningless term. What we're talking about is slave-owning society. That's what ties these thirteen or so states together. They at least have that common bond. The diversity of their experience in terms of settlement is the best example of the differences between these states. We have areas that have been settled now for two hundred years and areas that have been settled for two years. We've got a high newcomer population as opposed to a well-settled population.

ED AYERS   Something I have to remind people about is that when we talk about the Old South, a large part of the Old South in 1859 is about the age of a subdivision that's outside Richmond today.

GREGG KIMBALL   And then, of course, there's this huge country and mountainous South that extends all the way from Georgia up through western Virginia. There you have subsistence farming to some extent, somewhat isolated, although there is a lot of debate about how much market penetration there is in those areas.

ED AYERS   We've already established that most people in the North are farmers as well.

BOB KENZER   Right. Yes.

ED AYERS   Would there be much difference between a Northern farm and a Southern farm with non-slaveholders?

BOB KENZER   Size. Southern farms are two to three times larger in size. And that makes sense. You can't have three hundred acres under cultivation with just a white family, say, a father, mother, and two, three, four, five children. You need a slave population. You also need the density of the population. You take any county, for example, in Pennsylvania, an agricultural state that is often compared with Virginia, and the population density is so much higher in the northern countryside.

ED AYERS   That's because of slavery?

BOB KENZER   Because of the absence of slavery.

ED AYERS   How would the lives of the three-fourths of white Southern families not owning slaves have been affected by living among some slaveholders?

CHARLES DEW   The average Southern farmer is a yeoman who owns his own land and works it with the help of his family; he might own a slave. But they have something in common, which is white skin. If you are white in the antebellum South, there is a floor below which you cannot go. You have a whole population of four million people whom you consider, and your society considers, inferior to you. You don't have to be actively involved in the system to derive at least the psychological benefits of the system. The South as a whole sees a cloud on the horizon, and it's called the Republican Party. The Republican Party is born in 1854 in response to the Kansas-Nebraska Act and the whole question of the repeal of the Missouri Compromise and what's going to happen to these territories that we've gained from Mexico. The South sees the Republican Party, for the first time, as a political institution that's sectional, that is hostile to slavery; and if it is ever empowered, it is going to be a threat to the South's economy, to its culture, to its society, to its white civilization.

ED AYERS   But in their only election so far, in 1856, the Republicans did not do very well.

CHARLES DEW   But in 1858 the Republicans added eighteen seats in the House of Representatives, and they were scoring victories in places that the Democrats knew they had to win, like Pennsylvania, in order to carry the election. The only way Buchanan won in 1856 was to carry a solid South and a tier of states that bordered on the South. The Democratic strength in those border areas is eroding as a response to this bitter contest over what's going to happen to slavery in Kansas.

ED AYERS   So once again, I'm confused. You have slave profits that have never been higher, cotton prices have never been higher. The South is being settled at a remarkably rapid rate, as fast as the North?

BOB KENZER   No.

ED AYERS   Why is the South not being settled as fast as the North?

BOB KENZER   Largely because of immigration into the North. If they opened up the slave trade again, of course, it would have been. But the immigrant population that's flooding into the North in late '40s and early '50s, and continues on, guarantees that the North is going to grow. As I said, the population of Virginia grew 12 percent in that decade, the United States as a whole grew about 36 percent, and the Northern population about 40 percent.

ED AYERS   Why don't Irish and German immigrants come to the South as much?

BOB KENZER   They have to compete against slave labor, particularly the Irish.

GREGG KIMBALL   They are coming. One of the interesting things about Henry Wise, the governor of Virginia, is he's starting to play very strongly to white working-class people in his appeals. He wrote several tracts attacking the Know-Nothings, and he makes a speech in 1858 when Monroe is brought back and reinterred in Hollywood Cemetery, basically saying that the day of the old aristocracy is over. We need mechanics, people who can really create a dynamic state. He reads the handwriting on the wall. After the '51 constitution, all these white working-class guys can vote. I think there is a transformation, not as rapid as in the North, but definitely a transformation.

ED AYERS Is there a lot of political conflict inside Virginia? You've got what becomes West Virginia over there. What does it have in common with Tidewater?

GREGG KIMBALL Not much.

ED AYERS But you also said they can't vote for these Republicans?

BOB KENZER Right. But in the Upper South, here in Virginia in particular, in North Carolina, in Maryland, there's an active two-party system. We don't have a Whig Party anymore, but they're not voting Democrat. They're still voting for an opposition candidate. That's what they call themselves, The Opposition. This is in contrast to the Lower South, where by this point the Democrats are getting 70 percent of the vote in states like Alabama, where there had been a very active Whig Party. I think that's terribly important to understand, and it may shape the future, because Upper South residents are used to a competitive two-party system in which one party may be in power one year and may lose power the next. They may view a national election differently from people in the Lower South, who have come to see how one party can dominate.

ED AYERS Are white Southerners generally worried?

CHARLES DEW I think those who are politically aware are, and a lot of people are politically aware because they read newspapers. Incredibly, a newspaper will pass four, five, or six hands and be read avidly, column after column of very small print. They will know William Henry Seward gave a speech in Rochester in 1858 in which he talked about an irrepressible conflict between the slave South and the North. Seward is widely expected to be the Republican nominee.

GREGG KIMBALL There's a wonderful moment when, in August of '59, a group of militiamen from Richmond go up to New York, reciprocating the Monroe event in '58. [The New York Eighth Regiment served as a guard of honor at New York's City Hall when Monroe's remains were disinterred, and the New York Seventh Regiment escorted the remains on the trip to Richmond.] It's all about the bonds between them and the great middle of the American population that agree on everything. The crazy abolitionists and the fire-eaters are causing the trouble. But we know, because we have those bonds of fraternity, that we are all Americans and we understand what that is. So again, is that denial? They clearly understand that these issues are out there, but there's a feeling I get from reading their letters and diaries that they belong to this great middle, and they believe that can be preserved.

ED AYERS   The lower band of Northerners who voted for Buchanan think that great middle is what's going to hold the country together, no matter what may come.

BOB KENZER   Right. And there's reason historically to believe that's going to happen. There have been compromises so many times, with Missouri and then in the 1830s and again in 1850. If you were somebody who was saying, "I see a cataclysm in the future that we can't avoid," I think most Americans would look at you and say, "Haven't we always avoided them before?" So, yes, it may be a different sort of potential threat with this new and growing Republican Party, but ultimately, I think it is true that there is this sort of middle band. I think Virginians, and Richmonders in particular, feel this more than elsewhere because they are more economically tied to the North than the Deep South is. And they know, ultimately, if there is a cataclysm, it's going to hurt Virginia a lot more than Alabama.

ED AYERS   So a confusion again. It sounds like the South is participating in telegraphs, in railroads, building very rapidly, right? All these newspapers are going around. That sounds like progress to me. Why doesn't this progress, why doesn't this connection, tie the North and South together more?

GREGG KIMBALL   Sometimes the connections have a negative impact. For instance, there's a wonderful letter by a merchant from Richmond who took a railroad trip to New York. He starts polling people about the coming election. As he goes farther north, he starts to realize that there really are people who are going to vote for the Republican Party. By going to these places, he starts to understand.

ED AYERS   The more they know each other, the more they know how different they are.

GREGG KIMBALL   Yes, I think so. There are comments where people say that Richmond has become a Yankee town.

CHARLES DEW   And never forget the power of a single cataclysmic event. If you had read Seward's irrepressible conflict speech, and then Harpers Ferry comes a little later in this year of 1859, when someone comes down with an armed band, including Negroes, you're going to feel that a prediction is being realized—that what Seward had talked about in 1858 has the potential to become a reality.

ED AYERS   The title of this session is "The Future of Virginia and the South." I'd like each of you to tell me how different Virginians would have imagined the future. Lauranett, what do people held in slavery imagine the future looks like?

LAURANETT LEE   Certainly they hope that they will be released from this bondage. There is a very strong religious sentiment, an oral culture where they quote scripture from the Bible. They can imagine that one day they will be free. Looking at what is going on with the increasing slave trade, it would be hard to imagine that, but there is always hope.

GREGG KIMBALL   I see a rise of mass political culture, the continued growth of immigrant populations that politicians will have to pay attention to, and a continued growth in the industrial sector.

ED AYERS   So people look to Richmond and see the future of the South in some ways: the adaptability of slavery, the adaptations to modern life, the world's increasing reliance on slaved-produced products, whether wheat or cotton of the South. Generally, if you are a white Virginian, a white Southerner, there is no real reason to be unduly concerned. There have been political problems there all along. If you're a black Virginian, it is hard to see anything that's going to change things very radically any time soon, but you will keep working for it every day on an individual basis, a family basis, and in your heart.

LAURANETT LEE   Very much.

First Question-and-Answer Session

for "Taking Stock of the Nation in 1859"
and "The Future of Virginia and the South"

Participants in the question-and-answer session were Christy Coleman, Charles Dew, Gary Gallagher, Walter Johnson, Robert Kenzer, Gregg Kimball, Lauranett Lee, and Joan Waugh, with Edward L. Ayers moderating.

ED AYERS   The first question is from Katherine Wright. She asks, "You spoke on women abolitionists. Can you speak to the other end of spectrum, Southern proslavery women activists?"

LAURANETT LEE   As a matter of fact, abolitionists didn't come out and say that they were abolitionists. There were unfortunate incidents of people, white people, being whipped if they claimed that they were abolitionists. There are women who begged the court not to whip them because they and their children would be outcasts in the community. Proslavery women were a large part of the community. The women who were slave mistresses would want to keep that status. It's part of being in an elite group. As is true in our society, many were involved in conspicuous consumption. Having enslaved people is part of being one who is conspicuously consuming part of the culture.

CHARLES DEW   I would say race trumps gender in this context. I remember a single letter I read that struck me as the most powerful statement of that I had ever seen. It was written by a woman out in the valley whose mother had died, and her mother's estate had to be settled. That meant, perhaps, the sale of the slaves. She wrote her husband, who controlled this process, and said, "I raised these children," and she named them, and talked about what she had done. She had sewn for them. She had nursed them back to health when they were sick. And she said, "Black children have to be looked to just as white children." And then she said, "Why did I do this, my husband?" She said, "I did it for my children so that my children would inherit these children." In a single moment she had gone from being a woman and a mother to being a slave mistress, looking out for the well-being of her children by passing these slaves to them. I think that's eloquent testimony to what Lauranett was talking about.

JOAN WAUGH I'm not sure that you can compare a group of anti-slavery or abolitionist females in the North with another group that would come out in public in such a way in the South because of the differences in the way that each society was organized. I know we've talked about a lot of things the North and South had in common, but one of the things they did not have in common was the role for public women that was gathering steam throughout the nineteenth century and was in full steam in 1850s. For example, women were hired as teachers in the North. That wasn't commonly true in the South. Even though it remained controversial for women to speak in public in the North, they still did. They were also very active in their churches, coming from the church-based movement to reform movements, such as temperance societies. Many women ran those kinds of societies in the North. I don't think you had that in the South.

GREGG KIMBALL The closest thing I can think of is some of the women novelists in the South who implicitly defended the Southern plantation order in their writings.

ED AYERS Related to that, Scott Hanson asks, "Besides the Grimké sisters, were there other Southern women who advocated an end of slavery?"

CHARLES DEW If they did, they left the South, like the Grimkés.

WALTER JOHNSON We could also think about African American women as Southern women who are antislavery. If we broaden what we mean by "woman" in relationship to the South, and what we mean by antislavery in relationship to active resistance, then we would have a different answer to that. We would have Harriet Tubman, Sojourner Truth, and countless lesser-known figures.

GARY GALLAGHER I think a few statements have been pulled out of diaries and some letters and used too often to argue that many slave-holding women were secret abolitionists. Mary Chesnut is the most obvious one. That one line from Mary Chesnut is quoted again and again and again.

ED AYERS What was that line?

GARY GALLAGHER It's an antislavery line, or you can interpret it as an antislavery line. But when you look at the diaries, almost any of the other published diaries of slaveholding women, you certainly don't pick up that attitude.

CHARLES DEW And Mary Chesnut argued that the female victims of slavery were white women, not slave women.

ED AYERS The line was something like, "White women look around their dining room and see children that look like their husbands."

LAURANETT LEE Patriarchs of old.

ED AYERS Glen Crawford asks, "What were the consequences of the church's acceptance of slavery in the South? Was there ever a time when the churches did not accept slavery, and what was that history?"

CHARLES DEW There was a time.

GREGG KIMBALL Certainly the Quakers are an excellent example of an antislavery religious group that was quite vital in Virginia. But again, the issue is they left. Most of them left after the Revolution and early national period because of the tightening of the laws of slavery.

CHARLES DEW And there's a difference between the eighteenth and nineteenth centuries. The Baptists and Methodists had an antislavery tradition in the eighteenth century. Slaves were incorporated into the churches and given a voice; so were white women. Gradually toward the end of the eighteenth century, those churches were becoming increasingly female and African American. The ministers started worrying about this, and they started preaching a more muscular Christianity that said that women have got to retreat back to the domestic sphere. As you get into the nineteenth century, you find them embracing both slavery and patriarchy and seeing them as part of the same cultural phenomenon.

ED AYERS So in some ways, the churches became more conservative.

CHARLES DEW They did.

ED AYERS So by 1859 there was really no dissent within the churches, and in some ways the churches became ever more institutionalized. Someone mentioned earlier the division between the Northern and Southern branches of major Protestant churches.

CHARLES DEW   They were the first institutions to break.

ED AYERS   When was that?

CHARLES DEW   It started in the 1840s. By 1860 the only one that held together was the Episcopal Church, because they had a hierarchy, and—

GARY GALLAGHER   The Catholic Church.

CHARLES DEW   And the Catholic Church. I was thinking Protestant denominations. But the Presbyterians, the Methodists, the Baptists all split.

GREGG KIMBALL   We didn't mention that some of the earliest settlers in Richmond were Jewish. There was a thriving Jewish community here and in many of the Southern cities. They seemed to have been so well integrated that they also accepted slavery as a normal part of the order of the society in which they lived.

LAURANETT LEE   Also, when I think about the Quaker influence, I think about Robert Pleasants of Henrico County, who freed many enslaved people. Ironically, last week a historic highway marker was erected at 20th and Main Streets in Richmond regarding Quaker activity. In 1859 that area would have been part of the slave trade.

ED AYERS   There are records of free blacks owning slaves and bequeathing them in their wills. Can somebody explain that to us?

BOB KENZER   One of the difficulties here in Virginia and in other Southern states was that laws had been passed stating that once enslaved individuals became freed men or freed women, they would have to leave the state. And so a significant number of African Americans owning slaves—not all, by any means, but a significant part— kept their relatives in a state of quasi slavery to avoid the problem of having to be separated because of the law. The laws being passed by the state legislatures created part of this condition at least.

ED AYERS   But would we have had African American slaveholders who bought enslaved people the way white people did?

WALTER JOHNSON   I think we need to address that forthrightly. I think there were free people of color who were slaveholders. I don't think that perfidy or class privilege is limited by racial privilege, by skin privilege. But I think that once we deal with that forthrightly, there's a tendency then to start to imagine a world that is like *Gone with the Wind* as a minstrel show, and all of a sudden all the slaveholders are black. That is not the case; we are talking about a very small number of people. There are complex relationships to family and to the question of deportation. And there are also people who owned people of their same race and exploited them in many of the same ways present in cross-racial slavery.

ED AYERS   So there's no law against it?

CHARLES DEW   That tends to be more in the Deep South, Louisiana. I think Bob's right that, for Virginia, it would be a man buying his wife and children to keep them as part of his family.

ED AYERS   Or vice versa, the wife buying her husband, if she had access to the money, being a domestic—

CHARLES DEW   That would be the Virginia way.

GREGG KIMBALL   That recognizes that the caste system among African Americans is different in a place like Louisiana than in Virginia.

ED AYERS   Mike asks, "How do I tell the difference between a free black and a slave that I meet on the street of Richmond?" That's a great question.

LAURANETT LEE   You would not be able to tell.

CHRISTY COLEMAN   Not by looking, no.

LAURANETT LEE   Free blacks were required to carry their papers with them. But they could still easily be kidnapped and sold into slavery.

BOB KENZER   But there are some demographic factors to consider with what the census will call the mulatto population. A much higher share of that population is free than the black population. In South Carolina half the mulatto population is free, whereas only 2 percent of the black population is free. In the Upper South, especially, free blacks are more likely by white perceptions to be a light-skinned population. In the Deep South, particularly in Louisiana, that's not necessarily the case.

LAURANETT LEE   And you do have the mulatto population who choose to leave Virginia. The Gilliam family of Prince George County, for example, was light enough to pass for white. Once they moved, they did pass for white.

ED AYERS   I guess that implicit in this question is that freed black people would not be permitted to dress up too much.

CHRISTY COLEMAN   Some of them did. It depends on the amount of wealth or relative wealth they had. They were interested in buying nice hats or a nice suit. One of the mainstays of the popular culture of minstrelsy was making fun of the fact that free black African Americans would go through this ritual of dressing up on Sunday and putting on their finest and going out. They would make fun of that.

On the question of skin color, there was a Frenchman who made the comment that when he was in Virginia in the 1820s, most of the enslaved population was black, talking about very dark skin color. He comes back twenty-five years later and he's astonished—most of them he describes as yellow. An amalgamation has taken place here. I'm not sure that you would, in fact, be able to physically tell the difference. There is a lightening of the African skin, and certainly you do have a larger percentage that is mulatto. But guess what? That mulatto population is then marrying, connecting back with darker African Americans. It starts to balance itself.

GARY GALLAGHER   Ed, coming back to wealth and apparent wealth, I think visitors to New Orleans would have found a quite vibrant and substantial free black community.

ED AYERS   So the answer is that the way someone dressed would be your best indication.

GARY GALLAGHER   It would be a key.

CHRISTY COLEMAN   But not the only one.

ED AYERS   Rose Powell asks, "How much of a factor was the North's use of cheap immigrant labor in moving the region away from slavery?"

BOB KENZER   I think very little. I say that because the movement away from slavery in the North begins in New England with the Revolution. So we're talking about many, many years before the immigration begins. Now, some of the Northern states take longer, New York most notably, but the steady movement in the North against slavery is really an outgrowth of the Revolution. It's not in any way tied to the large immigration that occurred in the 1840s and early 1850s.

CHRISTY COLEMAN   I would add the simple point that the other thing about the North that's distinctly different is that its economy is not built on the slave system. It was much easier to break away and to wrap their ideologies around these revolutionary themes. It wasn't as difficult to make the break and create emancipation or gradual emancipation as it was in the South.

CHARLES DEW   I would add to a point that Joan made earlier. The abolition numbers in the North are minuscule, and the vast majority of Northerners despised abolitionists. William Lloyd Garrison was dragged through the streets of Boston by a mob with a noose around his neck, and they came close to stringing him up. I think when the Irish, particularly, came into Northern cities and began competing with African Americans, real hostility developed. In the riots in New York City in 1863, the Irish played a very important role, and African Americans were the target of a lot of their violence.

ED AYERS   This feeds into another question, from Joe Knox: "Did the abolitionists care about the deplorable labor conditions in the industrial North?"

JOAN WAUGH   The abolitionists, generally, were from the heart of the capitalist class. They were passionate advocates of free labor. There have been studies suggesting that most abolitionists came from manufacturing families or families that owned businesses, and they celebrated free labor, or at least the possibilities inherent in the free-labor system. So I would say, no, they weren't as critical of Northern labor conditions.

ED AYERS   The abolitionists and unionists were different groups with different agendas.

WALTER JOHNSON   You might want to imagine a whole spectrum of views of what the term "freedom" might mean. I think the question implies that there can be a foreshortening of the notion of freedom down to the right to work in a crappy situation for a wage. One might argue that what the Civil War would produce was a very foreshortened notion of freedom. One might include a notion of freedom that also has political rights, the right to intermarry. One might include a notion of freedom that has a genuine focus on human equality and cross-racial flourishing. I think all of those different notions of freedom are present in the antislavery movement. But I think I agree with Joan that those who have a generally egalitarian focus on multiracial flourishing in the United States of America are a distinct minority. Those who believe that the right to work for a wage is an acceptable notion of freedom, well, I think there are a lot of those folks.

GARY GALLAGHER   And the right to work for a wage would not have been cast in terms of having a "crappy" job all your life by most people. I think those who embraced the free-labor ideology really did believe that it somewhat obscured the line between those who own and those who labor with their hands and do nothing else, that crossing over really was possible. Rising politicians in the 1850s, including the loser in the senatorial election in Illinois in 1858, functioned as perfect examples of that—someone who starts having control only of their labor and ends up with a substantial position.

ED AYERS I think that it was a common point made by proslavery folks that the antislavery advocates in the North did not seem to care very much about workers in the depression of 1857.

GARY GALLAGHER George Fitzhugh and others hammered on that. You care so much about slaves, but what about in Pittsburgh—

ED AYERS The people right next door to you.

Larry Evans asks, "Were there whites in the South who had enough money to buy slaves, but chose not to? If so, roughly what percentage of whites made that choice?"

CHARLES DEW I think there were those, certainly, who felt that way. But I think the model of aspiration was to buy slaves because that's how you began climbing the social and economic ladder.

ED AYERS Could you become wealthy without being a slaveholder in the South?

CHARLES DEW Yes, you could, but I think it was easier to use slave labor as your principal way to get there. I recall a wonderful illustration of this point about Southerners and their attitudes toward slavery: A very good historian out at Stanford spent a year reading manuscripts from Chapel Hill and Durham and so on. He was looking for dissenters, people who cut against the grain. And he was particularly looking in the antebellum period for Southerners who criticized slavery and stayed in the South. He found about half a dozen, they were all ministers, and they all kept their doubts confined to their personal diaries. And I've often thought that was pretty eloquent testimony to the embrace of this institution, even by those who were not directly affected by it.

ED AYERS So a key component of all that, though, is we would assume there would have been quite a few white Southerners who did not want to be slaveholders and just left. Because we had millions of people, white people, leaving the South before the Civil War, right?

CHARLES DEW   Absolutely.

WALTER JOHNSON   I have one thing to add to what Charles said. What does wealth mean in the South? What wealth means is enslaved people. It's not simply that enslaved people are labor. Enslaved people are the dominant form of capital formation. Slavery is bound up with the ability to borrow money. When we talk about the slave trade, one of the ways that people get into the slave trade is that slaves were offered as collateral for loans. Indeed it's enslaved people who provide a lot of liquidity in the economy as far as lending because it's a much easier form of collateral to sell off than land. One of the things that you would have to look at is how are you going to get wealthy if you're not participating in the dominant modality of capital formation?

GARY GALLAGHER   The migration goes both ways, however. There are also a lot of people from free states coming into the slaveholding states with no problems about the institution of slavery and making their way. It really is going both ways. I think it's also important to remember that we fall into a lot of traps in talking about the North and the South, or the free states and the slave states. Democrats make up a huge percentage of the people in the free states, and you would have found virtually no problem with the institution of slavery, as an institution, among them. So the fact that a white person leaves the South because he or she does not like slavery doesn't mean they're going to a place where everyone's going to pat them on the back and say, "Glad to have you with us now."

JOAN WAUGH   The political mix in Illinois, Indiana, and Ohio is characterized by the in-migration of substantial numbers of Southerners who left not because they hated slavery but because they felt their future would be improved elsewhere. And then they voted proslavery Democrat from there.

ED AYERS   That leads to our next excellent question, from Kendall Sterling. He says, "The 1850s saw the beginnings of a middle class in the South." I think that's true, certainly in towns and cities. "Did they resent the economic and social power of slaveholders?" And I would add: Did they buy into slavery? What would a middle-class slaveholder look like?

CHARLES DEW   A fascinating part of the Southern political culture was the degree to which it was not an aristocracy. It was a functioning nineteenth-century democracy with universal manhood suffrage being present almost everywhere. But your political leadership came by and large from the ranks of the small slaveholders. One historian in particular has looked very carefully at local and state officeholders in the South and at the secession conventions in 1860, and he doesn't find aristocrats, with twenty or more slaves; he finds middling-level slaveholders, with five to ten slaves.

ED AYERS How many slaves would the average slaveholding family own?

BOB KENZER Well, the most common is one, the second most common is two, then three, then four.

ED AYERS So "average" is a misleading concept?

BOB KENZER From the white perspective, most slave owners only have one, two, or three slaves. From the slave perspective, most are held in holdings of more than twenty. It's a very different way of looking at the same equation.

GREGG KIMBALL Because a lot of these middle-class folks are urban people, probably the majority of the slaves are going to be domestics, which we haven't really talked about. There's an entire domestic slave environment in cities that is not that dissimilar to the situation on the plantations. Someone like Horace Kent, who's actually a New Englander, the biggest dry goods merchant in Richmond, is going to own six or seven slaves that are primarily going to be domestics.

ED AYERS A question from Tom: "Why would the British want to destabilize the South if it was their primary supplier of cotton? Were they trying to establish their own colonies to grow cotton?"

WALTER JOHNSON In order to give a good answer to that question we would have to think very hard about what is meant by "the British." We would want to disaggregate antislavery philanthropy from British banks, which are very, very heavily invested in the South and the cotton trade; from British manufacturers, who might be very, very interested in the cultivation of other sources of cotton; and from British governmental and imperial officials, who might want to vertically integrate the empire. That might be the beginning of an answer.

The other part of the answer would be to say that it may not be the case that proslavery political economists always operate with those distinctions. I think that proslavery political economists see a very simple argument, which is in line with Fitzhugh's. They believe that slavery is actually the best way of organizing labor in the world. They believe that the British are, in their colonies, practicing slavery under another name. Therefore, the British so-called philanthropic effort to combat slavery elsewhere in the world is actually a cover for their own bonded labor practices. Now, in one way, that's a difficult proposition to argue for. I mean, one would not want to defend the labor practices of the British Empire. But for proslavery political economists, I think there is a tendency to try to imagine almost a coherent conspiratorial approach on the part of the British.

ED AYERS   People have been suspicious because Britain would have been the superpower of the mid-nineteenth century. They resented its ability to dictate the economy and politics of the world, and the United States had not forgotten the Revolution.

The final question is from Shirley Donovan: "Do you think citizens on the eve of the Civil War saw themselves primarily as Americans or as members of different ethnicities and races? What about blacks in regard to that question?"

GARY GALLAGHER   That's a question that comes up all the time. The historian David Potter gets at that point. People have an array of loyalties. I think different of those loyalties percolate to the top depending on the moment and the situation. That would be true among white Southerners. Take Robert E. Lee, for example. He has a loyalty to the United States, he has a loyalty to Virginia; it goes in many directions, and at different points, different ones are more important. I think that would be true very, very widely.

LAURANETT LEE   I think many African Americans here saw themselves as Virginians. They were very rooted to Virginia.

ED AYERS   They'd been here for two hundred years by 1859.

Harper's Ferry insurrection, from *Frank Leslie's Illustrated Newspaper,* November 5, 1859, p. 358. (Library of Congress, Prints and Photographs Division)

3 MAKING SENSE OF JOHN BROWN'S RAID

Presenters were David Blight, David Reynolds, Manisha Sinha, and Clarence Walker, with Edward L. Ayers moderating.

ED AYERS Unlike other sessions, this one deals with a story, a bounded series of events in space and time. We'll begin by telling the story of what we think of as John Brown's raid and then radiate out into understanding where it came from and its consequences.

DAVID REYNOLDS The Connecticut-born John Brown, who hated slavery from his youth onward, became one of the first abolitionists to take up arms against slavery before the Civil War. On October 16, 1859, he led a party of twenty-one to Harpers Ferry, Virginia, including five African American soldiers, to free the slaves of that area. He chose the location in part because it was a federal arsenal, and he wanted to make use of the weapons that he captured there.

They did capture Harpers Ferry and freed a good number of enslaved African Americans in that area, who came to his side. Some of them fought with him; others were given spears to guard their former masters while John Brown carried out his raid. However, he stalled too long in the fire-engine house of Harpers Ferry and did not escape to the mountains, where he had planned to create a kind of zone of terror by spreading groups of slave liberators through the mountain range that stretched deep into the South. He retreated to the engine house, where on October 18 the local militia and then Robert E. Lee with the federal troops trapped and ultimately captured him. Seventeen men, including ten members of Brown's force, were killed;

John Brown was wounded severely. He was held in the Charles Town, Virginia, jail and brought to trial on three counts: murder, conspiring with slaves to rebel, and treason against the State of Virginia. On October 27 his trial began, and five days later he was found guilty on all counts and was sentenced to hang. On December 2, 1859, he was executed. That's the fundamental story.

MANISHA SINHA   It's interesting that we are celebrating the life of a man who committed treason against the State of Virginia. But besides the bare-bones story that we know, the assumption is that slaves did not actually respond to John Brown's call for rebellion. I think, as David Reynolds's work and other new research have pointed out, that involvement among enslaved people in Jefferson County, Virginia, and in Maryland, and also among free African Americans, was far greater than was let on at John Brown's trial, and that many of these people simply faded away into history. Now we are digging to see exactly how many were actually involved in the raid, knew about it, and helped sustain it for a little while, from October 16 to 19 when it took place.

ED AYERS   So all we know is that there were more than five African Americans involved.

MANISHA SINHA   A recent estimate by two young scholars is that nearly three hundred African Americans were involved.

DAVID BLIGHT   I don't think we would want to slight the fact that John Brown's plan at Harpers Ferry was a military disaster. I think we also have to account for the fact that there are really good reasons that African American slaves around Northern Virginia and elsewhere were so suspicious of him. There are things we need to remember, apart from Virginia's official rhetoric, about why blacks didn't join. The explanation was typically slave loyalty: of course they didn't join; they were loyal to their masters. But a larger truth there is that most slaves, as in most slave populations in world history, were always suspicious of their would-be liberators because would-be liberators usually got you killed.

Also John Brown was, in many ways, a lousy strategist in the sense that he did not lay the groundwork very effectively for what he was hoping to do. Whatever we think of his motives and his actions, he hadn't really laid the groundwork. Even if there were three hundred people who were aware that he was up in Maryland planning this, he had not made his plans known to them, even though he had plenty of time. I wouldn't want to overemphasize the idea that there were a vast number of African Americans waiting for John Brown to arrive, because most of them had never heard of him.

CLARENCE WALKER   I would say that in the six-county area of Virginia and Maryland around Harpers Ferry, there were something like 18,000 slaves. Of that number, only about 5,000 were men and boys. This was a very mature slavery. It was small scale. It was not large plantations. These people wanted to be liberated, but I do not think this was a case where they were willing to spring forward and join. We know from studies of slavery that where you have large numbers of women and children, men are very cautious about what they're going to do. This was not Haiti in the eighteenth century. It was not the Palmares in the seventeenth century in Brazil. This was the United States, in which black people existed as a black island in a white sea, and that sea was heavily armed here in Virginia. So that may have been one of the reasons, if not the primary reason, for the caution on the part of the black population.

MANISHA SINHA   Yes, I think that's absolutely right. To a certain extent, the raid was suicidal. Whether that was planned or not is another question. A lot of people refused to join John Brown precisely for that reason. Frederick Douglass refused to join him because he thought it was a suicidal venture and would not work. In fact, we do know that slave rebellions, in general, are difficult to plan because the more people who know about it, the easier it is for it to get out and be informed on. That's exactly what happened to Gabriel's conspiracy right here in Virginia. Nat Turner's rebellion, the least planned one, was extremely successful, precisely because not many people knew about it. What we now know about John Brown, which is so interesting, is that his plan of spiriting away slaves to the mountains and forming a subterranean passageway to freedom was built on an entire decade of black activism of fugitive slaves who had run away from the Upper South and free blacks and abolitionists who helped them along the way. The tendency is to see the John Brown raid as an aberrant one, but if you put it in the context of the 1850s in terms of fugitive slave escapes and abolitionist help for fugitive slaves, you can see it as somewhat of a culmination of those events.

DAVID BLIGHT   One of the most vehement debates among abolitionists, black and white, but particularly among black abolitionists throughout the 1850s, was whether and how to use violence as a method. Many abolitionists who cut their teeth under William Lloyd Garrison, or as a Garrisonian, called themselves nonresistant (we'd call them pacifists). But by the 1850s there was a very rich debate in this hothouse of politics about how or if or where violence would ever be a useful tactic. Frederick Douglass himself had come to openly embrace violence as a means against slavery. He had to make a personal choice whether to go with Brown or not. If he had, we wouldn't be talking about Frederick Douglass very much except for his first two narratives.

DAVID REYNOLDS   I want to defend John Brown as a strategist. I think that his basic strategy was actually very smart and very good. If he had stuck to that strategy, who knows what might have happened. He had been a surveyor. He knew the mountain terrain well, the kind of caves that were there and the hiding places. He told Frederick Douglass, "These mountains were placed here to aid the emancipation of your race; they are full of natural forts, where one man for defense would be equal to a hundred for attack, where a large number of men could be concealed and baffle and elude pursuit for a long time." The mountains ran 2,200 miles from the North into the Deep South. On the one hand, some African Americans would go north if they didn't choose to join him, but then a good number would join him, presumably, as groups of people—we could call them cells today—in the mountains that descend into the very Deep South. From the mountains, they would launch nocturnal raids that then would prompt more terror and create a sense of fear and panic.

There was nothing the South feared more than slave rebellion. Ever since Nat Turner's rebellion in 1831, that was a subterranean panic or fear on the part of Southerners. John Brown wanted to tickle that fear through his plan of hiding out in the mountains. The basic strategy was sound. Why he stalled, that's the big question mark in history. If he hadn't stalled and had escaped immediately, followed out his plan, found those hiding places and then continued southward, evading would-be captors, I think there's some possibility that he would have created a huge panic throughout the South. Who knows exactly what the South would have done? He expected the South to want to compromise on slavery, to just say, "This is too much now. This is exploding all around us. We don't like this anymore. We're willing to compromise a little bit with the Republican Party." Who knows exactly what was going to happen when that happened? But I think he could have created a state of terror in the South.

DAVID BLIGHT   He'd read and studied about Maroon communities.

CLARENCE WALKER   The Maroons are the slaves who rebelled in the eighteenth century in Jamaica. They retreated into the mountains of Jamaica, where they then raided down on the plantations. But I think it's a mistake to see the Maroons as representing some kind of pan-black or pan-African sensibility, because we know from recent studies of Maroonage that many of the slaves on plantations hated the Maroons. They hated them because they took their women, they took their food, and they treated them insultingly because they had not rebelled. I'm not so sure that the model of Maroons in eighteenth-century Jamaica would have spoken to the condition of slaves in 1859.

DAVID BLIGHT   But as a military model, it was useful for John Brown to think about. If you're going to have a slave rebellion, you go to mountains. That was the one model he had.

MANISHA SINHA   If I may interject, the Maroons had signed a treaty in which they agreed to return runaway slaves. That may also have been a source of tension. But I think this is an important point, and the point is that we should cease looking at John Brown as an isolated event. He is extremely conscious of a long history of black resistance to slavery. That is the tradition that he identifies with. Not with the antislavery society and its emphasis on moral suasion and religious perfectionism.

ED AYERS   On the tradition Manisha talked about: It occurs to me that the three major slave revolts in American history all take place in Virginia. You spoke of Gabriel's rebellion in 1800 in Richmond, and then Nat Turner, in Southampton County. It's interesting that the Upper South is the place where rebellions occurred, and maybe not surprising when you think of it in those terms. You could argue that tradition showed that it was fruitless to try to rebel because both of those insurrections ended in mass executions, even of people who were only marginally involved. What lesson would Brown have drawn from the history of black rebellion in the country?

MANISHA SINHA   This is really the birthplace of slavery, so not surprisingly some of the most dramatic instances of slave resistance took place in Virginia. And of course, if you look at the Stono rebellion in South Carolina and the 1811 uprising in Louisiana, Virginia still ranks ahead. The question of black resistance is extremely important in understanding John Brown. In 1848 he paid to have two calls for slave rebellion published by the black abolitionists David Walker and Henry Highland Garnet. He was a great admirer of Toussaint Louverture and the Haitian Revolution. The Haitian Revolution was a source of inspiration because it is the only instance of a successful slave rebellion in world history. We know that he read about Spartacus because he talked about Spartacus and his military strategy. He explained to one of his comrades why he thought Spartacus was not successful. Besides that, he was very involved in another tradition of black activism, resistance to the Fugitive Slave Law. I think David Blight brought up an excellent point about this debate over violence in the 1850s among abolitionists. Some are talking about it as self-defense. This is how Douglass comes to accept violence: "If a slave catcher comes to get me, I will defend myself. He will be dead."

DAVID BLIGHT   For a slave, that's crucial.

MANISHA SINHA   And there's a turn in the movement, even among Garrisonians who are willing to take up arms against federal marshals and slave catchers. Of course John Brown was a part of this milieu. Immediately after the Fugitive Slave Law was passed in 1850, he started the League of Gileadites in Springfield, Massachusetts, with forty to forty-five African American men and women. Then in Kansas, of course, where he's known for some controversial acts, he liberated eleven slaves and sent them to the North through the Underground Railroad. One of these slaves had a child en route and named him John Brown. So if we understand John Brown in the broad context of slave resistance, and even free black resistance, to the events of the 1850s, whether it was the Kansas wars, the 1850 Fugitive Slave Law, or Dred Scott later on, he doesn't seem that aberrant.

ED AYERS   So what you're saying is that there are very deep roots and traditions across Western history and all across American history, and he was a self-conscious student of those traditions. Let's talk about John Brown the man.

DAVID REYNOLDS   He was born in Connecticut, but he lived for a long time in Ohio and Pennsylvania; he ended up living in Springfield for a while, and then North Elba, New York, where he settled among a colony of fugitives up there. He chose to live among the African Americans to try to help them.

ED AYERS   When would that have been?

DAVID REYNOLDS   He went up there in 1849. He's buried in North Elba. He was a devout Calvinistic Puritan. In a way he was a freak of nature because you would think that Christianity would automatically give rise to antislavery. For some people, that's true. But actually, probably numerically, it gave rise to a defense of slavery in the South even more than it did abolitionism because the Bible is full of slaveholders, and the South really believed they were being very Christian by introducing Africans to Christianity. They were saving the barbarians and all that. John Brown and his whole family were deep-dyed Christians who mutated in a very militantly abolitionist direction. When Brown was twelve, he saw an enslaved African American boy who was being beaten with an iron shovel and other household tools. From that date, he said, he became "a most determined Abolitionist," leading him to "swear eternal war with slavery." And he devoted much of the rest of his life to thinking about enslaved African Americans.

ED AYERS   Where would that scene of the beating with a shovel have taken place, David?

DAVID REYNOLDS   He was driving cattle for his father from Ohio to Michigan and lodged for a time with a man who owned a slave. He was totally disgusted when this young African American boy who had befriended him—an intelligent, personable young man—was made to sleep in the cold in rags, while he, as a white person, was invited to sit at the table with the master.

CLARENCE WALKER   I don't want to disagree with what David had to say, but I don't think he was a freak. For his age, if you're going to talk about the context, he was an exceptional person in terms of his racial attitudes. Unlike many abolitionists, he was not condescending to black people. He lived among black people, he worked with them. He wanted to adopt, I think, a black child into his family. He went to black churches, on one occasion giving up his pew in his church and sitting in a place that had been designated specifically for black people and allowing the black people to move forward and sit in his pew.

Brown, like William Lloyd Garrison or, say, Theodore Weld and Angelina Grimké, was truly a person who believed in interracial fellowship. This derives, as David pointed out, from a deep religiosity. Brown's family did not undergo that mutation that occurred in nineteenth-century Evangelical Protestantism where it softens itself from the strict Calvinist tradition. He continued to adhere to an older belief in a God who is omnipotent and omnipresent and who believed in justice. In 1859 he believes he is acting as an agent of that God when he comes to Harpers Ferry to liberate these slaves. What gets him into trouble in some ways is that he's so bounded by his religious sensibility that he does not take the opportunity to get out of the armory and do what he had planned to do.

DAVID BLIGHT To grasp what he did at Harpers Ferry, much less Kansas and in between, we really have to get our heads around his Calvinism. He believed in a kind of government of God more than a government of man. He believed in things like innate depravity. He believed in providential signs. He believed that God had a design for history, and God had agents acting in history. He thought human depravity was a natural part of human beings. His first allegiance—and he said this a hundred different ways—was to his sense of God's justice, not man's justice. God's laws, not man's law. It's the main way one can begin to think about how he developed self-justification.

MANISHA SINHA Brown was always known as the "Old Puritan" because he believed in this vengeful, wrathful God who would smite down sinners. He saw himself as an instrument of God, which sounds odd to us, but he truly seemed to believe that. I recently discovered that not only was Brown aware of all these incidents of slave rebellion, but some of his favorite books included the biography of Oliver Cromwell, books on the Roundhead tradition, the English Revolution tradition, the Protestant Puritan tradition. The Protestant *Book of Martyrs* was one of his favorite books. When he lingered in that engine house, I wonder whether he thought that his martyrdom, which is the way his death would be perceived by some people, would actually play a bigger political role than perhaps escaping and managing to ferret a few slaves out of the South.

DAVID REYNOLDS It is my belief that at some point that night, he decided he wanted to become a martyr. And he did become a martyr because he did live. In jail, he made many statements against slavery and said things like he would be far prouder to be accompanied to the gallows "by barefooted, barelegged, ragged slave children and their old gray-headed slave mother" than by any slave-supporting minister. All these abolitionist and racially progressive statements sounded so crazy then, and yet they slowly worked their way to the North so that he became a kind of Christian saint to certain Northerners who said, in effect, "Now, wait a minute. This is amazing that he feels this way."

DAVID BLIGHT He writes about a hundred letters during the one month he was in jail. If ever there was a case in history where the accused about to be executed, in a very, very public way, got to write his own epitaph, it is in the letter he writes his wife saying, "I will be far more valuable dead than I ever was alive." I always wondered, what does she think about that?

DAVID REYNOLDS "I am quite cheerful in view of my approaching end," he said, "—being fully persuaded that I am worth inconceivably more to hang than for any other purpose."

CLARENCE WALKER He was the father of something like twenty children. Eight of his children died in either youth or infancy.

DAVID BLIGHT Some through horrible accidents.

CLARENCE WALKER Two of his sons died at Harpers Ferry. He did not share in the expansiveness of the Jacksonian period, in the sense of progress and optimism that seems to have characterized the lives of lots of people. I think he took refuge in a deep religiosity. This religiosity was such that he may not have expected to succeed.

DAVID BLIGHT Isn't this partly why we still have such a problem with him?

ED AYERS What happened after Brown left North Elba?

DAVID REYNOLDS In the mid-1850s he went out to Kansas, which was poised between being admitted into the Union either as a slave state or as a free state. A bunch of easterners, including John Brown, went out there to try to prevent it from going for slavery and coming in as a slave state. It was called "Bleeding Kansas" because there was ongoing warfare there. It was dripping with blood; there were all kinds of pitched battles between free-state and proslavery people.

The reason he's controversial is that one night he led a party of eight men who took proslavery supporters out of their cabins at midnight and slaughtered them with swords. It's a horrible act that's not defensible; however, research has shown that of the thirty-six political murders committed between 1855 and 1858 in Kansas, eight of them were committed by antislavery people, including John Brown's five. The remainder were committed by the proslavery people. Some proslavery people in Kansas were known as border ruffians because they came across the border from Missouri, a slaveholding state, seized the polling booths in Kansas, and elected a fraudulent proslavery legislature in Kansas that was validated by the federal government. In the South there was a code of honor that included duels. Andrew Jackson was in three duels; he had bullets in his body. He was sort of a typical Southerner in that way. Henry Clay was in duels. Along with the code of the gentleman went a belief in violence. Several journalists said, "Aha, John Brown has brought Southern tactics to the Northern side."

A second thing I want to point out is that, yes, he did direct the murder of those people, and it was a horrible act, but some people say, "What would he have done with jet airplanes?" And I say that he would not have used jet airplanes. There were men and children and all ages of people in those cabins. He only selected the members of the proslavery party. In other words, he was much more selective than using a jet airplane as a weapon or exploding a bomb at Oklahoma City, where babies died. It wasn't like that. You can't say it was the same thing.

MANISHA SINHA The so-called Pottawatomie Massacre committed by John Brown, the five proslavery men he killed, must be seen in the context of the immense violence taking place in Kansas at this time in 1856. It is the height of the Kansas wars, maybe a kind of a prelude to a bigger conflagration. But it is important to remember that although the so-called border ruffians from Missouri were constantly invading Kansas and voting illegally to try to convert Kansas into a slave state, all these pro-Democratic, pro-Southern governors who came to Kansas, some of whom were slaveholders themselves, insisted that Kansas should, in fact, come out as a free state because they knew that the numbers were against them. The proslavery side tried to sort of force the issue through violence and through bizarre laws protecting slavery in Kansas, which would make it a crime even to speak out against slavery, and which meted terrible punishments on slaves if they attempted to escape from slavery. That is the context in which John Brown is operating. Remember, when he saw that young black boy being beaten with an iron shovel, he's supposed to have pledged eternal war against slavery. When John Brown said "eternal war against slavery," we know he meant it literally because of the Pottawatomie Massacre.

DAVID BLIGHT I would argue it's an act of war in a vigilante, guerrilla war. Within that context, we can come to understand it. Eye for an eye, tooth for a tooth, which he believed. A key point here is that the Pottawatomie Massacre and the battles that flowed from it, and Bleeding Kansas of that summer of 1856 into '57, is where John Brown's reputation begins to grow in the abolitionist communities in the East, and all over the country to some extent. There's this mystery about this man. Who is this John Brown? Who is this old guy with his band of followers who seems to be part of that guerrilla war out there, and yet he seems to keep escaping? So there's a mystique that grows about this man. A lot of those New England abolitionists who were going to give him money to develop his Harpers Ferry conspiracy don't want to know what all the facts were about Pottawatomie because it's better that they don't know.

CLARENCE WALKER But there was something horrific that went beyond the imagination in the Pottawatomie Massacre. To be sure, people were being killed, as Manisha and David have pointed out, but those people were not hacked to death. There is this vivid image in the press of men and boys being chopped up by knives or swords that creates, as David says, John Brown's reputation. It makes him a man of action for a bunch of New England intellectuals and others, and it just terrifies people in the South because they see in this the specter, possibly, of some kind of broader uprising.

ED AYERS How could he do this and not be caught, still be famous and going around and talking with people?

MANISHA SINHA He actually escaped. There was a price on his head, and he escaped and came back northeast and they never managed to catch him.

DAVID BLIGHT More than once. He goes back to Kansas and escapes again.

MANISHA SINHA I guess that was part of the mystique. But again, let's go back to the Pottawatomie Massacre—and that was a term, of course, that the proslavery side put to it. It is true that it took place in the context of all that guerrilla warfare in Kansas. But we have to remember that Brown, as Clarence pointed out earlier, identified with the suffering of slaves, with the trials of black people, to an extent that is somewhat unimaginable for a lot of people living at that time. Douglass said that Brown was the one white man who he felt had the iron of slavery pierced into his soul, as most black people did. When Brown declared war on slavery, I think he was more than just an ordinary free-state immigrant to Kansas fighting against proslavery forces. He sees slavery as a state of undeclared war against people of African descent. When he says, "I will carry that war into Africa," right before Harpers Ferry, it suggests the mindset with which he's operating. It is not to excuse what he did, but it is to try to understand what he meant; that he would wage a relentless war against slavery.

DAVID BLIGHT   The question of how he could do this and get away with it and why his reputation would grow is a complicated problem. But it boils down to this: there are a lot of Northerners—not just abolitionists but Northerners beyond abolitionism, and that's what's important here—who live in a Romantic age. They need a Romantic hero. John Brown, especially if you don't know all the details, is that kind of hero who may go and do what a lot of people wish might get done but could never think of doing themselves. And he becomes an agent of a kind of imagination about violence in a Northern community of reformers, antislavery folk, abolitionists, even some politicians, who are beginning to believe that slavery may have to have a violent end, somehow, someway. They don't have a clue how.

DAVID REYNOLDS   Henry David Thoreau became the biggest supporter of John Brown—Thoreau who had been a nonresistant. He had become famous for his views on civil disobedience. His essay would influence Gandhi, influence Martin Luther King Jr., and a whole bunch of passive resisters. Thoreau said that right-minded people must honor an antislavery warrior like John Brown, "even though he were of late the vilest murderer, who has settled that matter with himself." This was a complete flip-flop for Henry David Thoreau from nonresistance to his complete admiration in even admitting that possibly John Brown was a murderer.

ED AYERS   Did women admire him as much as men did?

DAVID REYNOLDS   Quite often, yes.

CLARENCE WALKER   But I think also the fact is that Brown—as I think Manisha pointed out—is not only identified with slavery. To him it's not an abstraction. It also grows out of his extreme disgust and repulsion at the treatment of black people in Northern society. For black people, the difference between slavery and freedom, if you look at it on a continuum, wasn't some sort of abstraction. The two interacted with each other. Brown saw this daily. He moves to North Elba, where Gerrit Smith has established this colony called Timbucto, where black people live marginally in upstate New York.

DAVID BLIGHT   On terrible land.

CLARENCE WALKER   He sees the day-to-day humiliation and discrimination that takes place in Northern society and is directed at the free black population. For him this is not something happening farther away. It is a part of his day-to-day life when he's in the North.

DAVID BLIGHT   Is it fair to say that John Brown may have spent more time in his life in black churches or with black laborers and farmers than he ever did with sophisticated white abolitionists?

DAVID REYNOLDS   Absolutely.

MANISHA SINHA   We know that the abolition movement was an interracial movement, and the land that John Brown and African Americans settled in North Elba was donated by Gerrit Smith, the abolitionist leader from New York.

But you asked the gender question. We know, of course, that John Brown has often been portrayed by his biographers as this great patriarch with twenty children, two wives—the first died, and his second wife was Mary Brown. And we know that he seemed to be somewhat traditional in gender roles in his private life. Interestingly enough, he always referred to Harriet Tubman as "he," not as "she." He called her "General Tubman," which I've always wondered about. Did he think that women could not take on that activist role that Tubman had taken on?

DAVID REYNOLDS   Supposedly he went to a few women's rights lectures. I got the impression that, at least abstractly, he defended women's rights and also Native American rights. He was initiated in a play ceremony to a Native American tribe when he was young. Then when he was older and he was a farmer, a neighbor came to him and said they should take their guns and drive away some Indians who lived nearby. Brown glared at the man and said he'd rather drive him away than the natives. He really sympathized with the oppressed, people who lacked rights. That included women. Yes, he filled a kind of traditional, patriarchal role on the one hand, but at the same time he had such incredible admiration for Harriet Tubman. He idealized her almost as much as he idealized anybody that I know of, really.

ED AYERS   Let's zoom in now on what we think of as John Brown's raid. So he's been on the run, in and out of Canada, upstate New York, and Kansas. When he decides that Harpers Ferry is the place to begin the end of slavery, what is his planning, his thinking?

DAVID BLIGHT   By any legal definition, John Brown created a conspiracy. He was raising money, he was accumulating weapons. He was recruiting men, soldiers, including Harriet Tubman. He held a convention up in Chatham, Ontario, which was supposedly to attract his band of followers, his warriors. But he was very secret about it. He even drafted a provisional constitution. This has always been, to me, one of the most fascinating and bizarre things about John Brown. He drafts a provisional constitution for the State of Virginia that could be instated after he took over Virginia, after taking over the federal arsenal, by whatever means that was supposed to happen. And yet very few people seemed to know the details of what he was going to do, including Frederick Douglass, in whose home he lived for a month. Douglass knew where, and a little bit about how. But very few people were brought into his circle of exactly what his plan would be. He had wanted the raid at least a year earlier but had to postpone it. He postponed it because he wasn't raising enough money.

DAVID REYNOLDS   He didn't have enough support, financially and particularly in the number of people. The Chatham convention didn't produce enough soldiers for him. One African American from the Chatham convention came with him, but then scores of others did not come with him.

DAVID BLIGHT   He was hoping for hundreds, right?

DAVID REYNOLDS   Absolutely.

ED AYERS   Did he ever think about pulling out when he saw that he was only getting nineteen men instead of hundreds?

DAVID REYNOLDS At the end he was just going to do it. They camped out in Maryland for a while. A fair number of recruits came there. In October of 1859 he made that move. As David said, though, his plans were actually quite vague in the end. We don't really know what, in the end, his plans were. Originally, as I said, he wanted to escape to the mountains. I wish we knew on a day-to-day basis toward the end what he was actually thinking.

ED AYERS Do we have a sense that his young confederates knew they were getting ready to walk into the slaughter, and they just did it with him, or did they have confidence that he was going to think of a way to bring it to a successful conclusion?

MANISHA SINHA It's interesting because they sort of defend him, those who survived the raid. The first account of the raid is written by an African American, Osborne Anderson: *A Voice from Harpers Ferry.*

DAVID BLIGHT He was the only black to survive.

MANISHA SINHA The other four perished during the raid. They all defend his plan of action. It's not clear exactly what Brown intended. What is clear from his letters is that he only wanted to free the slaves. If there was a plan, it was more like Nat Turner's, where a few would begin the raid and many more would join. It was not like Gabriel's conspiracy or Denmark Vesey's conspiracy in 1822, in South Carolina, which is now being debated by historians, which presumably involved thousands of slaves, and therefore was leaked out and the authorities were informed. These people were caught and hanged or transported out of the state. His model seemed to be that of Nat Turner. Brown admired the Haitian Revolution, which began as a slave rebellion and then just spread. I think that if there was a model of resistance, maybe that was it, rather than the subterranean plan. In his last letters, he keeps talking about, "My only aim is to free the slaves." And then he realizes that once it has failed, the one way he could still achieve his objective was to make himself a martyr to the cause.

DAVID BLIGHT Don't we know enough to know that he actually had real political plans out of this? It wasn't just to be a bloodletting. He wanted to take over Virginia. As bizarre as the plans were, he had political plans.

MANISHA SINHA Absolutely. I think the provisional constitution is interesting because it gives the right to vote to men and women, and it talks about holding property in common, not individual property rights. So again, a very interesting abolitionist.

ED AYERS What is the story of the actual moment of confrontation?

DAVID REYNOLDS What happens is that John Brown goes out or sends some people out to the local area to free some enslaved African Americans and bring them back to Harpers Ferry. They do that, and they come back with certain white masters who are being held captive by the black people. And John Brown kind of waits. He stops a train that's going through, but he makes the mistake of letting the train continue. And, of course, the train passengers told the people at the next stop what was happening. He should at least have held the train there for a long, long time until his men had escaped and he went up to the mountains.

ED AYERS There's that modern technology again, the train and the telegraph.

DAVID REYNOLDS Soon it's all over the telegraph wires. By morning, the local militia had moved in. Within a day, Robert E. Lee and his troops came from Washington. There was a pitched battle. Two of John Brown's sons were killed. John Brown himself should have been killed, and, if he had died, then he probably would have had very little influence on history. Thoreau said that it wasn't his action but his words after his action that made any difference. His words *after* Harpers Ferry were much more powerful than any bullets fired *at* Harpers Ferry.

DAVID BLIGHT And the hanging.

DAVID REYNOLDS But what had happened at Harpers Ferry is that Lieutenant Israel Green had picked up his dress sword that day, and he stabbed John Brown six times with this flimsy sword. As it was, Brown was pretty seriously wounded, and he was on his back during the trial, lying on a cot. He should have been killed, but by mere accident, he lived. And he lived to write and speak those eloquent antislavery words, and then act the way he did on the gallows, where he turned and thanked his jailer, a slaveholder, for his kind treatment. He was very kind to all his slaveholding captors. It was the system of slavery he wanted to crush, not the slaveholders themselves.

ED AYERS The obvious question would be: Why would the State of

Virginia permit him this stage, to send out all these letters, and to say all these things?

DAVID BLIGHT   If this were after 1859, I think we could say they would rue the day they hanged him; however, it's not. They tried him for treason, slave insurrection, and murder.

ED AYERS   What was their logic by going through with this trial?

MANISHA SINHA   I think Henry Wise, who was the governor at that time, personally admired Brown. Wise was pretty proslavery in his attitudes, we know. He thought that he would be displaying slaveholder benevolence, I guess. It was like the trials that slaves sometimes got. It seemed to have procedural fairness, but we all know that the decks were stacked.

ED AYERS   So it's a way to show that even with this, the State of Virginia is not going to just execute somebody, but they're going through the law.

MANISHA SINHA   Give him a show of a trial. Remember, one of the first slaveholders that Brown tells his raiding party to go to and take hostage is the great-grandnephew of George Washington, Lewis Washington. He takes the sword that Frederick the Great gave George Washington. He tells the slaves of Lewis Washington to do this, and they join him. He's aware of the symbolism of Virginia. So is Wise. And everyone thinks it's going to play in their favor. Unfortunately for Governor Wise, it played in Brown's favor.

DAVID REYNOLDS   Virtually everything that Brown said in jail was recorded by Southern journalists. They printed it because it sounded so crazy to them. He's defending the rights of African Americans and racial integration. It was so obviously crazy for that day. Particularly in the South they said, "Sure, we'll publish it." It's kind of like the tabloids. And then a few abolitionists started looking at this guy twice and soon were comparing him to Jesus Christ. Meanwhile, he kept getting reported because the Southerners thought that he was just so nuts in his views—

ED AYERS   —that he would undermine the abolitionists' cause. Give him enough rope, so to speak.

CLARENCE WALKER   He undermines it quite simply, by leaving behind this trunk with his correspondence in it, which points to all of his connections in Northern society. It raises in the South the speculation that they're all lunatics. Who is he talking to? Gerrit Smith, Theodore Parker, Thomas Wentworth Higginson, George Luther Stearns, and the husband of the woman who wrote the "Battle Hymn of the Republic."

MANISHA SINHA Samuel Gridley Howe.

DAVID REYNOLDS And Frederick Douglass.

CLARENCE WALKER What it shows is that this guy had been able to implicate large numbers of the Northern intellectual aristocracy.

ED AYERS So Virginians and Governor Wise let this play out because they thought it was to their advantage to do so; it wasn't some slip?

MANISHA SINHA No. Remember that John Brown was interviewed by Senator James Mason and Clement Vallandigham. Though they tried to implicate him by his own words, he ends up rising to the occasion and defends himself rather eloquently.

DAVID BLIGHT I don't think the State of Virginia could have possibly avoided doing what it did in that moment. This was an attempt at massive slave insurrection. This was a raid on a federal arsenal. It doesn't get any worse than this. Given the politics of that moment, which we haven't discussed that much, I don't see how they could have done anything differently. A crucial thing here, again, is this was a sensational event, probably like no other that had occurred in American history. The press coverage of this is beyond anything that had ever happened. It's the original show trial of American history. The press has the capacity with the telegraph to report the facts occurring.

MANISHA SINHA This is how Brown gains victory from failure.

ED AYERS What's the response in the North?

CLARENCE WALKER Well, at first people are sort of shocked, and they don't actually say that they condone this. Slowly but surely, the population shifts to make Brown a hero.

ED AYERS Why? What changed?

DAVID REYNOLDS Partly it was the transcendentalists, who had idolized John Brown for a long time. Ralph Waldo Emerson declared in a big speech in Boston that Brown would "make the gallows as glorious as the cross." Emerson was like the philosophical leader of the nation. And here's Ralph Waldo Emerson comparing him to Jesus Christ? Henry David Thoreau went all over Massachusetts, and his "Plea for

Captain John Brown" said, "He could not be tried by his peers, for his peers do not exist. . . . I rejoice that I live in this age, that I was his contemporary." So these two heavyweight intellectuals come out on his side. And as Clarence mentioned, more and more thinkers and reformers in the North climb on the John Brown bandwagon, whereas the initial response, as was mentioned, was pretty negative both North and South. You have this growing movement so that by the time of the Civil War, a certain body of troops from the North would march South saying, "John Brown's body lies mouldering in the grave, but his soul keeps marching on." By that time, he becomes a cultural icon.

DAVID BLIGHT   Louisa May Alcott said that Brown was like a perfectly blossoming rose. That's never worked for me. He wasn't a perfectly blossoming rose. I would just add that I think the most important ultimate reaction across the North is this deeply Christian reaction to John Brown. John Brown on the gallows became an American crucifixion. There's no question about that in the way people received it. The most important reaction, ultimately, is the way Republican politicians have to position themselves.

MANISHA SINHA   There was a range of reaction in the North. Among African Americans, John Brown was revered as a hero right from the start. There was never a question about his madness. They saw him as the only sane white man around sometimes. Among abolitionists, he was revered as a martyr. Even Garrisonians and Garrison himself, who were pacifists, admired the fact that this man was ready to lay down his life for the cause against slavery. Then there were unionist conservatives, who had unionist meetings to try to prove to the South that they were not all followers of John Brown. Then, of course, there was the Republican Party, which actually, interestingly enough, tried to distance itself from Brown as consisting of moderate antislavery people.

ED AYERS   How can we characterize Northern reaction to Brown?

MANISHA SINHA   Most Northern towns rang their bells when John Brown was hanged.

DAVID REYNOLDS   By the time he's hanged in early December, I would say most Northerners sympathized with him.

DAVID BLIGHT   But they would do it in an interesting way. They would condemn the deeds and they would condemn the acts. But they would often do it in such a way as to shine the light on the problem of slavery. It's as though John Brown had done something that you know might happen in this country anyway.

ED AYERS   That sounds like pretty rapid transformation, in a matter of weeks. Before the hanging, the white North would not have supported John Brown and Pottawatomie and all that stuff, right? Then an immediate reaction to the raid was widespread denunciation of it, right? But then as a result of the trial and the letters, and the efforts by the intelligentsia of the North, in a matter of weeks, the North comes to believe that this is something admirable at some level?

DAVID REYNOLDS   It shows the effect of language. When people like Thoreau and Emerson used those words about John Brown, it's like the phrase "the shot heard round the world," the phrase Emerson had used about the American Revolution. That one phrase even today galvanizes people. "The gallows as glorious as the cross" went through the papers like a ricocheting bullet. People said, "My God," and started thinking about this. Maybe there's something to admire here, they began to think.

ED AYERS   What was the white South saying?

DAVID REYNOLDS   Oh, they hated him. They thought he was going to hell. Abe Lincoln would be on one side and John Brown would be on the other side of Satan.

MANISHA SINHA   If you read the Southern newspapers from the time, he's a criminal, he's a horse thief, he's a madman.

DAVID BLIGHT   He's a midnight terrorist.

ED AYERS   What did they think about his Christianity? Did they accept that?

CLARENCE WALKER   It was the product, quite obviously, of an insane mind that had perverted Christianity. Because only a lunatic would think of encouraging slaves to rise up and kill white people. This is just unthinkable. This is like the Haitian Revolution. Absolutely unthinkable.

MANISHA SINHA   Those Southerners who had been fighting for secession, particularly in the Lower South—not that many in Virginia— throughout the 1850s, used John Brown as a way to illustrate that this is what the North really stands for. They're going to kill us. They'll come in the middle of the night and cut our throats. They stand for slave rebellion.

DAVID BLIGHT The new political party that exists in 1859 is really an abolitionist party. If you scratch a William Seward, you get a John Brown.

MANISHA SINHA They called the Republican Party the "Brown-Helper party."

ED AYERS What did the Republican Party platform say about John Brown?

DAVID REYNOLDS Condemned it totally.

MANISHA SINHA Completely distanced itself.

DAVID REYNOLDS Ironically, the most admiring sentences were said by the Southerners at the very beginning who actually saw John Brown at Harpers Ferry. Governor Wise and others who saw him immediately said he was so incredibly cool and determined and brave. Later they rued their praise of him. They automatically thought that everyone would think his views were totally crazy. They admired someone that had his kind of gentlemanly code of honor, someone who was brave, someone who used violence to defend his principles. At the very, very beginning, the Southerners who witnessed him in person admired him as a person. Of course, slowly they realized that he was horrible in his ideas about slavery. They thought there was a whole Northern conspiracy behind him.

ED AYERS Do we think his timing had anything to do with the coming presidential election of 1860?

DAVID BLIGHT He wanted the raid even earlier. He would have done it at least a year earlier if he had had his act together.

MANISHA SINHA I think it allowed the Republicans to show the North the radical abolitionist way, the John Brown way, and then portray themselves as this moderate, antislavery, constitutional, politically legitimate party.

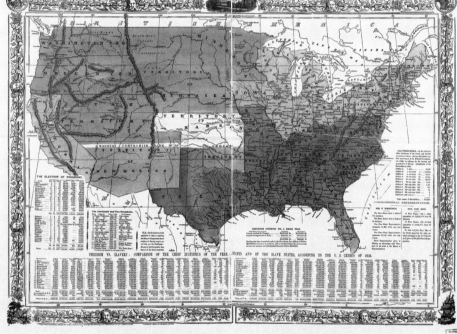

Reynold's Political Map of the United States, created and published by Wm. C. Reynolds and J. C. Jones. (Library of Congress, Geography and Map Division)

4 PREDICTIONS FOR THE ELECTION OF 1860

Presenters were Jean Baker, Daniel Crofts, Nelson Lankford, and Elizabeth Varon, with Edward L. Ayers moderating.

ED AYERS   This session's job is to predict an election a year out, from the perspective of 1859. There have been all kinds of changes in the last decade. How did we get to where we are today?

NELSON LANKFORD   We should put in a word for the Constitution of the United States. The Constitution was ambiguous on the nature of sovereignty. Once the states ceded their sovereignty to the nation, could they undo that ratification? That ambiguity meant that people of goodwill could argue over whether secession was a right or not. Union-loving people could, in their minds, think about undoing the Union without doing violence to that Constitution.

ED AYERS   Taking it back to the Constitution suggests that in the fundamental law of the land some issues are not resolved.

DAN CROFTS   I think we need also to recognize that the Republican Party and its leaders love the Union and the Constitution, and although they dislike slavery, they have ideals that are in tension with each other. The tension is something that we now perhaps can realize was insoluble, but they would like to have it both ways.

ED AYERS   Today the Republicans are called the GOP—the "Grand Old Party." But in fact, it was far newer than the Democratic Party. What are the dominant parties in the 1850s?

JEAN BAKER   Let's talk about the Whigs. Great name.

ED AYERS   Where does that name come from?

JEAN BAKER   The English. The Whigs were opponents of Andrew Jackson. There was a very stable party system that existed from the period of Jackson up into the 1850s. But in that decade we see something that had rarely happened in American history before—the deterioration and disappearance of a political party, in this case the Whigs. At the same time these new parties appear—one can hardly remember their names—the Free Soil Party, the Liberty Party, the Know-Nothing Party (there's a name for a political party!). So it seems to me that politics is in the air everywhere in 1859. The problem is, what's going to happen?

ED AYERS   So we have this Constitution, which is ambiguous. And then we have the Republican Party. And, finally, a stable political system has begun to unravel, and there's this proliferation of other parties. How did that come to be?

LIZ VARON   I would start by saying that the stable political system rests on a shaky foundation in the sense that there have been pervasive fears of the fragility of the republic, fears of the potential for disunion. Nelson alluded to the sort of constitutional ambiguities at the heart of those fears. One could say that Americans have, in effect, been haunted by visions of disunion since the founding. These fears took three forms. There were fears about moral decline, which republican theory had suggested since the time of the Greeks and Romans was something that republics in particular had to worry about, since they were based on the vigilance of their citizenry; fears of foreign intervention or foreign threats; and, lastly, fears of internal factionalism. All three of these kinds of fears gave rise to visions of disunion. Over the course of the antebellum period, these anxieties about disunion intensify and come to focus on the issue of slavery. For us, probably the most important proximate event in explaining this escalation to which we have referred is the Kansas-Nebraska Act because it gives to our political scene the nomenclature of the coming campaign in the concepts of popular sovereignty and non-extension.

ED AYERS   Is the Whig Party strong all the way up to 1854?

JEAN BAKER   They had won two presidential elections—William Henry Harrison in 1840 and Zachary Taylor in 1848. They ran a candidate in 1852 who might have won except for a third party. But they are in a state of deterioration. It's a mysterious thing that a political party that was so strong for this length of time would suddenly disappear. I believe that their problem was that as the politics of slavery came to take over the South, there was nowhere for the Whigs to go except to be strongly proslavery, which hadn't been such an issue in the 1840s. I think that they were isolated because of a shift in partisan positions in the South.

ED AYERS So you have two national parties, the Democrats and the Whigs, who ten years before were fairly strongly entrenched. You have Whigs being strong in Mississippi and Massachusetts, and you have Democrats strong in Georgia and Michigan, right? Is that what held the country together across all the tensions, Liz?

LIZ VARON To a certain extent. The Whigs have suffered, however, from a couple of setbacks, including the loss of two very notable leaders, Henry Clay and Daniel Webster. Both had positioned themselves as voices of compromise, and both had conjured disunion for the American population as a cataclysmic, terrible tragedy, something to be avoided at all costs. They had used this as a sort of political tool against their opponents on both sides of the political spectrum, trying to carve out a middle ground. They pass from the scene, and there's a lot of anxiety in 1859 that there are no leaders anymore who have skill and ability at compromise. The Whigs also lose some of their economic issues. They position themselves as the party of economic modernization. There are forces in the Democratic Party eager to co-opt some of those themes. Once the salience of these economic issues as the source of contention between the two parties fades, the Whigs are casting about for an identity and are less able to hold the country together.

ED AYERS Did the Democrats change?

NELSON LANKFORD The Democrats are, by this time, the one national party. They have a strong Northern and Southern wing. This new party, the Republicans, is only strong in the Northeast and the Midwest. The Democrats are the dominant national party, but you have to remember that there's this discredited Democratic administration now, the Buchanan administration. There is a campaign song his opponents used that goes something like, "How can you make a man stand up tall if he never had a backbone?" That's what people think of Buchanan. So on the face of it, they may look strong, but within the Democratic Party, the Southern and Northern factions are more at loggerheads. The Southerners want their party to defend Southern rights and slavery more than some of the Northern Democrats want to do. They may look stronger than the Whigs on the surface, but they have trouble within.

DAN CROFTS   Let's get a little more context here. As late as 1848 the Whigs won a national election. They ran pretty well in the North and the South, gaining enough states to win the Electoral College. But by 1852 they fell under quite hard times. They carried exactly two states in the North and two in the South. It was quite disheartening to their supporters. The situation didn't look like it was going to get much better. This tide of foreign immigration that we've been hearing about tended to bring to the United States people who were more likely to become Democrats.

ED AYERS   Why? What do the Democrats believe in?

DAN CROFTS   Democrats are more receptive to Catholic immigrants.

ED AYERS   Why?

DAN CROFTS   They promise to treat them civilly and not stigmatize them.

ED AYERS   Why would they do that?

JEAN BAKER   They want to take them to the polls. Perhaps this is the point to introduce this other party, aka the American Party. This was a party that played into immigration issues in cities like Baltimore, Philadelphia, et cetera. Today we call it "nativism." The idea was that these people were taking over America. These immigrants don't know anything about American customs. The Know-Nothings had an idea that the naturalization age should be raised to twenty-one years because, after all, that's how long it took an American from the time that they were born in the United States to get to vote.

ED AYERS   Unless you're a woman, and then it took forever.

JEAN BAKER   Yes—and not until 1920 do women get the vote. The other issue is Roman Catholicism. There is a real fear of Roman Catholics. I'm thinking of my home city of Baltimore. Suddenly Protestants looked around, and they found that Irish Catholics were building schools and churches. And guess what? They wanted to use their own Bible, the Douai Bible, in public schools. These were the kinds of themes that energized a group of Americans who began the new American Party.

LIZ VARON   There was a perception, and there was a lot of evidence of this, too, that the Democrats had looked at, for example, Irish immigrants, a population victimized by prejudice, and had seen them as a potential key part of the Democratic alliance. The Irish could be allies in the fight to preserve slavery on the grounds that a racial order that gives certain privileges to white men is something that might benefit these immigrants. There was a perception on the part of the American Party that these immigrant voters were becoming a critical swing vote that could really turn elections in Democrats' favor in crucial places.

ED AYERS   What I think I hear you saying is that some of these broad social changes that have been discussed begin to undermine the two-party system so that immigration undercuts the Whigs before they can struggle with some sectional issues.

DAN CROFTS   Dear old Winfield Scott, the Whig candidate in '52, went out campaigning and said that he loved that rich Irish brogue, yet that statement did him and the Whigs no good. The trend in immigration seemed to suggest that people who were not Democrats might be looking for a new political home, and indeed they soon were, for the reasons Jean has explained.

ED AYERS   Now I know that there was a Compromise of 1850 in all of this, which was sectional in some ways. So help me understand how you can have these currents of nativism and immigration and the abandonment of the Whig Party. I think what I would say is that the Whigs have been much more of an evangelical Christian party. The Democrats are like, "It's not our business to tell people what to do with their lives." So the Whigs have been far more inclined toward temperance and things like that. Is this fair to say? And the Democrats believe it is not the government's job to get into your business. If you want to be Catholic, that's fine. Go ahead.

JEAN BAKER   I think we jumped over the question, though, about the Democratic Party, which would seem to be the party of the future, wouldn't it? It's the only national party and the party that has the administration—James Buchanan. Besides the presidency, the Democrats also control the House and the Senate during this period. And they control a very important third branch of the United States government, the Supreme Court. So it would seem in 1856, when James Buchanan is elected, that the Democrats would be the party of the future.

ED AYERS   They have everything going their way, right?

JEAN BAKER   Yes.

DAN CROFTS   We need to plug in here the troubles that are occurring out in Kansas, which start in '54 and become worse in '55, and even worse in '56. This is happening at exactly the same time as the growth of this Know-Nothing or American Party that Jean has talked about. There are two forces at work, rather distinct from each other, that end up, in a sense, kind of scissoring the existing party system. By the midterm elections in 1854, there's a great deal of political upheaval both North and South, but especially in the North. The Northern Democrats take a huge hit in the off-term elections in 1854 because what was going on in Kansas was a big political liability for them. Their party was judged responsible for the mess.

ED AYERS   Why would this undermine the Democrats?

LIZ VARON   Let's just start by observing that the Democrats had promised to protect slavery. By the mid-1850s there's a division in Democratic ranks about whether the party should protect slavery and about whether it in fact can protect slavery. This is a big problem. Doubts about whether it should protect slavery come from an emerging free-soil wing of the party; doubts about whether it can protect slavery come from a militant Southern rights movement. Kansas proves to be so divisive. Stephen Douglas proposes the Kansas-Nebraska bill, which suggests that we could settle the sectional conflict through the mechanism of popular sovereignty. Let the people from the territories decide whether they want slavery or not.

ED AYERS   A very democratic idea: *You* figure it out.

LIZ VARON   Seems great. The problem is, in order for this to work, the various factions have to concede each other's legitimacy, and they have to have some belief and trust in the basic mechanism of the political system. What happens out in Kansas is that neither of the warring parties concedes the other's legitimacy, and neither has faith in the sanctity of the existing political system out there. Settlers rush into the territories, proslavery and antislavery. There's a lot of violence, though it's been trumped up. The images of Bleeding Kansas suggest hundreds of thousands of people dying. About fifty or so did. But the press makes a business out of blowing things out of proportion. Certainly, images of Bleeding Kansas are everywhere to be seen. Popular sovereignty proves not to work so well. It leads to bloodshed, and you have two governments in Kansas, each denying the legitimacy of the other, each vying for federal support. The Buchanan administration supports the proslavery one.

NELSON LANKFORD And the leading Democrat from Illinois is at loggerheads with the leading Democrat in the White House.

ED AYERS It sounds like a mess.

NELSON LANKFORD The Democratic Party is tearing itself apart.

ED AYERS It suggests to me that maybe it would be time to start a new party. The Know-Nothings, the Americans, collapse. They can't sustain their brief power. But there are all these nativist folks out there, there are all these people dissatisfied with the Democrats, and all these people looking for somebody to stand up against the militant white South.

DAN CROFTS The American Party looked very strong in '54, '55, and early '56, but the sectional North/South stuff hurts them. We had an American Party, otherwise known as the Know-Nothing Party, but they find themselves disagreeing about the appropriate policy on North/South issues. And so we end up with—get this—North Americans and South Americans.

NELSON LANKFORD If you take a step back, in Virginia there was a gubernatorial election in 1855. The Know-Nothings thought about this as a test case to become the next national party. Henry Wise was a Democrat, and he defeated the Know-Nothing candidate, Thomas Flournoy, who didn't campaign. Henry Wise initiated this new thing of a nonstop campaign tour. That's what defeated the Know-Nothings. The Know-Nothings took the wrong lesson. They thought that their defeat came because they were perceived as soft on slavery. They took that lesson to the national convention. They tried to deal with slavery to make themselves acceptable to the South. That, as Dan said, defeated their intention of becoming a national party.

JEAN BAKER I'd like to offer a halfway house for this whole process. We like to think in party labels. We're accustomed as Americans to a two-party system. But there was a process where, as Dan says, you moved out of the Whig Party, or perhaps the Know-Nothing Party, and you moved into this room that's called anti-Nebraskans. That goes to the critical crucible of the Kansas-Nebraska Act, which surely uproots all of these ancient allegiances. It's a surprising thing during this period because Americans join parties because they have inherited their party allegiances. And here we are in the 1850s, and what's happening? There are these strange names. There's the Opposition Party, there are the Anti-Nebraskans. There's something called the People's Party. It's during this process that, I believe, two things happen. One, this party that we're now going to talk about emerges; and the other thing is that the politics of America becomes focused on antislavery in the territories, which of course is the ruling slogan of the Republican Party. Northern Democrats move into the Republican Party. There's a famous story about Stephen Douglas, who is surely one of the leading figures of this period, and he's the head of the committee on territories. He goes to a meeting with President Buchanan, and Buchanan says, "You're going to have to support the party on what is called the Lecompton Constitution." And Stephen Douglas says, "I will not do this." Buchanan threatens and says, "You'll be ruled out of the party. Remember what happened to those senators in Andrew Jackson's time." Stephen Douglas turns to the president and says, "Mr. President, Andrew Jackson is dead."

LIZ VARON   Another way to think about this is to observe, as some commentators have, that American politics has a kind of paranoid style. People see conspiracies everywhere. This is related to our earlier discussions about fears of disunion. This was a time and place where to attribute to your political opponents not only lack of patriotism but treasonous motives, a desire really to bring down the Union, was not uncommon. There was a tendency to see conspiracies. The Know-Nothings proposed that Americans should be scared of a papist conspiracy. The Republicans suggested that what Americans had most to fear was a Slave Power conspiracy. It turned out Americans were a lot more scared of a Slave Power conspiracy than they were of an alleged papist conspiracy.

DAN CROFTS   There's also a key memorable moment that helps to bring this front and center to Northern voters. It's the same week as

John Brown's affair out in the dark of the night in Kansas at Pottawatomie, and far more visible. It was the assault on Charles Sumner
on the floor of the United States Senate. Sumner is sitting at his desk,
writing a letter. Preston Brooks from South Carolina, a congressman, steps up behind him and starts beating him over the head. This
resonated in a huge way across the North because it symbolized the
way in which militant Southerners were going to trample the rights
of free speech in the most sacred place of all, the floor of Congress.
Free white men of the North can't speak their own mind without fear
of being beaten senseless. That was just a few weeks before the Republican convention was going to meet. Right up until that point, you
probably would have said the Know-Nothings, the Americans, were
the stronger of the non-Democratic parties. But there's a huge turn-
around the last week of May, the first week of June. In the end, the
Republican Party swallows up most of these former Know-Nothings
in the North. You end up with a vigorous, though brand-new, political
party, which runs quite a successful race, not quite enough to win, but
sometimes called a victorious defeat. They carried eleven states in the
North.

ED AYERS   So you're saying Preston Brooks helps create the Republican Party?

DAN CROFTS   He certainly does.

ED AYERS   Let's be clear about this. The party had been formed in
1854. Only eighteen months later, it suddenly finds its prominence
elevated as a result of a series of events—Kansas-Nebraska, divisions
among the Democrats, Preston Brooks and the caning of Sumner, and
so forth. That's where we are in '56.

NELSON LANKFORD   You can't emphasize too strongly that caning
of Charles Sumner incident in Congress that Dan talked about. One
congressman referring to this event said that congressmen went to the
capitol armed. He said, "The only ones who don't go with a revolver
and knife are the ones who go with two revolvers." That was an exag-
geration.

JEAN BAKER   It's interesting in the context of Southern culture, and
I suppose, political culture, that Preston Brooks took a gutta-percha
cane and hit Sumner over the head. If this kind of hostility had occurred between a Southerner and a Southerner, we would have had

a duel. Hitting someone over the head with a cane was a sign of disrespect; you did not merit a duel. I think that this was one of several cultural differences pointed to by Northern newspapers, which covered this caning extensively. It changed lots of people's minds.

LIZ VARON   It gave a sort of grim salience to an argument abolitionists had been making for a very long time: that slavery is a kind of warfare, and that slaveholders, the Slave Power conspiracy, are willing to use any means, extralegal means and means of violence, to maintain the slave system. This seems to be a dramatic illustration of that.

ED AYERS   These things seem not quite accidental, but they're not growing out of a natural course of events, or are they? Are these things bound to happen or are they just the random things that make history move—contingency?

JEAN BAKER   I think these episodes are so obvious in the 1850s because we look at the 1850s so carefully to study the Civil War. But there is a great deal of attention paid at the time to things like this. There were plenty of duels. These are the kinds of things that are picked up by the press and everyone pays a lot of attention to them. We've heard about the newspapers. Horace Greeley's *New York Tribune* has a circulation of 300,000, and of course those newspapers were sent to others.

LIZ VARON   The newspapers made no pretense of objectivity. It's not as though they aimed at objectivity and fell short of the mark. They were openly partisan, and therefore they tended to raise the temperature of the public again and again and again with their coverage of these events.

NELSON LANKFORD   We tend to think that people have a short attention span in our own day. And they did, too. You think about it, the telegraph and newspaper were like the unsleeping Internet and 24/7 news. People learned information quickly, but they quickly forgot and moved on to something else.

ED AYERS   So the press was looking for new stimulation all the time.

NELSON LANKFORD   To follow up on what Liz said about the paranoid nature: Sometimes, as you know, paranoid people can be right that they're being followed. The Southerners believed there was an abolitionist conspiracy to attack the Southern way of life. The abolitionists believed in the great Slave Power conspiracy to take over the levers of the federal government or to use them to expand slavery. You can say these are extreme, but in some ways there's some truth in both.

ED AYERS How so?

NELSON LANKFORD We talked about the Democratic control of the White House. The Supreme Court was very conservative. The Republicans and the abolitionists looked at the power of the South, power that existed even as the demography was moving against the South. The North was growing and the South was to a lesser extent, yet the South seemed to have all these levers of power in Washington.

DAN CROFTS The Republican Party looked to become a more powerful force. They looked to politics and to the efficacy of elections and the normal political process. It's very important for us to keep this in mind because we're always in danger of being overwhelmed by hindsight here, of knowing what happens after 1859. We're looking at Republicans who think that it's time to knock down what they consider excessive Southern power in the Union. Their campaign rallying cry is free soil, free labor, free men, and they happen to nominate a candidate for president in '56 who is John C. Frémont. Free soil, free labor, free speech, free men, and Frémont. They are trying to take control of the federal government away from what they consider a corrupt Democratic Party that has fallen into the hands of proslavery extremists. And they're saying, "If you vote the right way, we can settle this thing." In '56, the Republicans did pretty well. They carried states in New England and they carried states out to the west where significant numbers of New Englanders had settled, but they didn't get quite enough to win. But they didn't miss by too much. The big states and the free states that they didn't carry were Pennsylvania and Indiana and Illinois. A little more Republican push in those states, and you could potentially elect a president, not in '56, but potentially four years down the road.

JEAN BAKER This is not unique to the Republicans. By the 1850s there's a party culture that involves a whole lot of specific activities that you do if you're a partisan. You may dress up in costume. You march in what are called companies. You have various symbols. You might go out and have what was called a pole raising. And then your competitors, with great glee, would go back and cut down your pole and then you would put it up again. Politics in this period is mass entertainment. There were these entrancing activities that you could participate in. And remember, this is a period before the Australian ballot, when you go to the polls and openly get your ballot with some sort of a symbol—and by the way, it's not an elephant or a donkey during this period. For the Democrats, it's a rooster. You place that ballot into a box. In some states, there's viva voce voting where you go and say out loud which party you support. There's an attachment that the Republicans are able to build among young voters. We see when we look at the statistics—this is hard slogging in terms of historical research—that it's young people that the Republicans are attracting throughout the North and the Midwest.

LIZ VARON   Let me add that the Republicans are building that consensus around a concept that on the face of it seems bloodless—the non-extension of slavery. They're not asking for the immediate abolition of slavery. They concede that slavery has the constitutional right to exist where it already does. They're asking that it not spread to the territories. They emerge as an anti–Kansas-Nebraska party, and it seems at first that they're going to stake their claim on the sanctity of the Missouri Compromise, that 36°30' line dividing North and South and free from slave. But soon they move to a different position in which they're reaching for an even deeper consensus, and that is what they believe to be the Founders' consensus that slavery should gradually wither away. They believe that if slavery is not allowed to spread, it will eventually become extinct. On the face of it, this doesn't seem like a great rallying cry. But the emotional purchase of this idea is that "we will no longer make concessions to slaveholders." This seems to slaveholders to be quite a strong stand.

ED AYERS   Do they believe that the slaveholders want to expand into Cuba and Latin America?

JEAN BAKER   Absolutely. This is one of Buchanan's major efforts. When he was the minister to the Court of St. James's in England, he wrote what we call the Ostend Manifesto, which said Cuba would automatically be a part of the United States. This ratcheting up infuriated Northerners because they saw that the Democrats were interested in expanding beyond the continental United States into areas of Mexico.

ED AYERS   When people imagine this conflict, they often say, "You obviously couldn't grow cotton in New Mexico, so what's the big deal?" But if we pull the lens back a little bit farther, we see there's a lot more at stake, and it's not just replicating what exists in Alabama and Mississippi. They can look at Virginia and see that slavery can do lots of things. They can look at Cuba and imagine what you could do with American slavery there. This non-expansion of slavery was very charged.

DAN CROFTS   It's very charged, but if you have a Republican president and perhaps at least a Republican House of Representatives, it's going to be pretty hard to acquire a new territory, even though the Senate, historically, has a more powerful role in things like territorial acquisition. The Republicans could say, "Vote the right sort of people into office, and this problem will solve itself."

ED AYERS   That's right. If you don't, you're going to be fighting a war to take these territories. In addition, in the Dred Scott decision the Supreme Court seems to contradict the Republican platform.

JEAN BAKER   The Dred Scott decision was a complicated decision in terms of who signed which part of it. The critical thing was that [Chief Justice Roger B.] Taney and the majority came down on the point that Dred Scott could not sue in federal courts. He could not become and was not at this time a citizen. The really horrible part of Dred Scott was that blacks had no rights that whites had to follow or support. This undermined, of course, all free Negroes, free blacks, in the United States. Their circumstances were now perilous because they could be sent back into slavery, which was the normal place that some thought they should be. Dred Scott is another one of those hammers. If we can think of the Union as a marble statue, this is another one of the cracks that comes. Of course Northern papers were infuriated by the Dred Scott decision.

DAN CROFTS   I think we need to make it clear here, just building on what Jean has said, that for Republicans, the most startling and unsettling aspect of Dred Scott is the argument that Congress has no power to restrict slavery from going into the territories, which was the least common denominator that held this brand-new Republican Party together.

JEAN BAKER   And it abolished the Missouri Compromise.

LIZ VARON   And this raises the specter of the nationalization of slavery. If slaveholders have a right to take their slaves everywhere, then perhaps they have a right to take them into the North and even into the states that have abolished slavery.

ED AYERS   So there are reasons, if you're a Republican, to look at this and see that the South is actually playing offense, quite effectively; they've got the Supreme Court, they've got the presidency, and they've got this booming slave economy. Although Republicans have all the populous states behind them, despite their showing in 1856, they feel that it's by no means clear that they're going to win.

NELSON LANKFORD   Nothing is inevitable. But you see why Southerners were very nervous. The Republicans fell short, but it wouldn't take that much to win. The Republicans could put together an electoral majority as a regional party, not picking a few states off across the country the way it was done before.

ED AYERS   Was this something new? Had there been a regional party before?

DAN CROFTS   There had never been anything like this. This was only in the free states.

ED AYERS   So the Democrats and Southerners say, "Well, this is a violation of the way the American democracy works. You line up, and you try to build coalitions." The Republicans are cheating by saying they're not going to even try to recruit votes in the South. It seems a violation of the fundamental precepts of democracy.

JEAN BAKER   There is a moment when the Republicans, at least in the Northwest, try to have an alliance with the Democrats. Really the point here is to attract Stephen Douglas, who is one of the key personalities in all this, because he is disaffected from Southern Democrats. We will all pull together, and we will have a party that may have to be renamed. But nonetheless, we'll have a majority. Many, many people in the 1850s saw what was happening. There's something like 300 electoral votes. And if you look at the map, you'll see that the Northern states, non-slave states, command 170 electoral votes. So what is the future?

LIZ VARON   But the Republicans have a big, big problem. For many decades, the Democrats have successfully used against the antislavery movement the argument that abolitionists are disunionists: that they want to drive a wedge between the North and the South, and they then want to use the alienation of the two sections as the pretext to wage a war of conquest and impose emancipation at bayonet point. The core of this argument is that Republicans are Garrisonians in disguise; that whatever they may say about non-extension and free soil, free labor, free men, and all the rest, in their heart of hearts they want to take the existing social hierarchy and turn it upside down. This is something that many Northerners fear. The Democrats have been playing on that fear for a long time, and the Republicans are keenly aware of the fact that they have to disarm the charge that they are disunionists. Abraham Lincoln writes in his personal papers, in effect, that "this is the objection that we have to find a way to answer."

ED AYERS   Who's this Abraham Lincoln guy?

LIZ VARON   He's the star of the West. He makes a reputation for himself in the Lincoln-Douglas debates, and he loses to Stephen Douglas in 1858. He doesn't win the election, but the press covers his performance, which is a very strong performance. He's aware of the trend that Jean talked about; that is to say, Douglas tries to give an antislavery reading for a Northern audience of his own popular sovereignty doctrine by suggesting that settlers in the territories, by refusing to pass slave codes that would protect slavery, can keep slavery out. This is meant to appeal to free-soil Democrats. Republicans worry that Douglas is trying to co-opt some of their message, and Lincoln sets himself up as a person who will expose the moral bankruptcy of Douglas's position. Lincoln says that Douglas is indifferent to slavery, and that indifference is a de facto endorsement because the Slave Power conspiracy is always on the move. So Lincoln makes a name for himself.

ED AYERS   How does Lincoln lose if he makes a name for himself?

DAN CROFTS   Lincoln and Douglas were running for the United States Senate before the twentieth century. So it was a decision to be made by the state legislature. It was an unusual situation where both parties long in advance indicated who their choice would be, but it was, in fact, an election from the state legislature. The whole House was being reelected, or elected, but some of the state senate seats were holdovers. The ominous thing for the Democrats is that when all the votes were tallied, several thousand more people had voted Republican in Illinois in these legislative elections even though there had been just enough residual Democratic strength for Douglas to hold his seat. Douglas is not just an ordinary Northern Democrat. He's the poster child for the Northern wing of the Democracy. He's their favorite candidate for 1860, and here's a guy who's hardly able to hold his own seat.

As far as the areas where Republicans are looking to pick up strength, one of them is the state of Illinois; next to it, the state of Indiana; and not least, the state of Pennsylvania. In 1858, the same time Lincoln and Douglas are running against each other in Illinois, there's a huge upset in Pennsylvania, which is the home of President James Buchanan. Republicans won a whole slew of seats in the House from Pennsylvania. They had done rather poorly in '56 and '57 there, but in '58 and then again in '59, Republicans in Pennsylvania downplayed North/South issues. They complained that the country had fallen into a nasty economic decline—this may sound familiar—and that the party in power was responsible for economic hard times. This played very well in industrial areas in the Schuylkill and Lehigh valleys.

The wave of the future, at least some Republicans thought, was to back away from North/South issues. In fact, the Republicans in Pennsylvania chose to call themselves the People's Party. They thought the Republican label was too polarizing and that there were many Northerners who didn't have any particular grudge against the South, but who wanted to get rid of the Buchanan administration.

ED AYERS Which was one they considered corrupt and ineffective, right? And then in the middle of this, we have John Brown's raid. How does it come in and what does it do to all this? This sounds really complicated—and I don't hear industrialization versus agrarianism in all this very much.

NELSON LANKFORD One narrative is that Brown's raid happened, the South was shocked and then relieved that masses of slaves didn't join. The people in the North were outraged, too, at the violence. It was only after Brown made these eloquent statements from prison and in the court that people in the North began to support him and there developed a groundswell of support for Brown by the time of his execution. I guess I have to disagree. People had a short attention span, and that groundswell declined in the North. People turned to other things. Brown was still a hero to the abolitionists, but one of the main things that Brown did politically was this: before Brown, the Opposition Party, the residual Whigs, and Know-Nothings in the Upper South were talking about negotiating with the Republicans and maybe providing some united opposition to the Democrats. John Brown killed that. The Old Whigs in the Upper South realized they could not talk to Republicans. One old Virginia Whig said he knew that Republicans weren't all bad abolitionists, but he said they were tadpole abolitionists that would grow up into the real thing. They went on their own, and that's why, as they go toward the election that produces the Civil War, we get an Upper South movement of the Opposition Party.

ED AYERS   What do the Democrats have to do to win this election of 1860 that's coming up?

DAN CROFTS   They've got to hold on to those states that they carried in '56. There were several states in the South that they won very narrowly because the Southern opposition was significant.

ED AYERS   It was the Old Whigs.

DAN CROFTS   The Old Whigs; they were called the American Party in '56 or the South American Party. They did carry Maryland, and they came very close in several other states, notably Kentucky and Tennessee. If they can add a few more, they are in a position to grab off a few of what had been Democratic states in '56. If you did not have a majority Electoral College, a presidential election goes into the House of Representatives. It was true then, it's true now.

JEAN BAKER   Jefferson Davis is smart enough at Vicksburg in 1857 to give a speech in which he lays this out. Southern Democrats will never win unless they attract some Northern votes, which can most successfully be done by nominating a Northern Democrat. Davis sees this so sharply. Of course, there are Southerners who want him to run for president; but he says he doesn't want to, which is what you had to do in the nineteenth century. There was none of this going out and saying, "I want to be president." But what Jefferson Davis suggests is that the Democrats run Franklin Pierce of New Hampshire as their candidate. It's surprising when we look back on this, but it makes sense. Pierce has been a president, he has a name. He might be able to save Pennsylvania, for example. But this does not happen.

DAN CROFTS   The Democrats have a huge problem. Their most popular candidate in the North is anathema in much of the South because he worked with the Republicans in 1858 against accepting Kansas into the Union as a slave state. And the spectacle of Stephen A. Douglas working day after day on the floor of the United States Senate with William H. Seward and several leading Republicans just kills them.

ED AYERS   So Douglas has been besmirched by cooperating. You need a stronger pro-Southern Democrat, right?

DAN CROFTS   And there are lots of would-be Southern presidential candidates who think their moment has come. Two of them are from Virginia: Henry Wise and Robert M. T. Hunter. There are the three Georgians. Good old Jeff Davis wouldn't have minded. The list goes on. If you don't nominate Douglas, you're unlikely to hold the states in the North that you've got to hold, yet the Southerners are adamant that they won't do it.

LIZ VARON   What does the Republican Party have to do? One thing they have to do is distance themselves from John Brown as fast as they can. They trip over themselves trying to do that. The problem is that William Seward had given this speech about an irrepressible conflict, which fed the Democratic accusation that the Republicans wanted war. Then along comes John Brown, and it is widely asserted in the South that John Brown's raid is the fruit of that irrepressible conflict speech. This tarnishes Seward, who had, going in, been the presumptive front-runner in the Republican pack.

ED AYERS   Who is he?

LIZ VARON   He is a New Yorker, a senator, a major architect of the Slave Power conspiracy idea. He had helped to give events in Kansas and Nebraska an interpretation that Northerners could latch on to, even if they weren't abolitionists. For example, he emphasized that what was happening in Kansas and Nebraska was a suppression of free speech, which was a dear and cherished right of Northern free men. He is now sort of tainted as radical. The Republicans have to cast him out and find someone who can make the case that they are the conservative party, conservative in the sense that they want to restore the consensus that slavery should gradually fade away.

DAN CROFTS   Abraham Lincoln says he simply wants to restore the policy of the Founding Fathers. The Founding Fathers were not happy about the presence of slavery. In Lincoln's eyes, the act of barring slavery north of the Ohio River, the Northwest Ordinance, provided a model that the country should come back to. By rescuing the country from the clutches of this proslavery Democratic Party, the free white men of the North would settle the situation, by means of an election, not by any violent means. Political legitimacy would be reestablished, and the country would be put on more solid ground than the shaky times it had gone through in the 1850s.

ED AYERS   We know that politics, now as then, is often about local issues, about bread-and-butter issues. We know there was this depression in 1857, hard times. Are there other issues?

NELSON LANKFORD   Let's look at Virginia. Virginia goes from the Atlantic Ocean to the Ohio River, borders three states. There is a great divide in Virginia. There are a million and a half people—half a million black, a million white. Most of the whites live west of the Blue Ridge, but they're underrepresented in the legislature. The Constitution of 1851 makes some concessions to them. But that division, that lack of equality of political power, which means unequal taxation, rankles the people in the west. And Virginia had almost split at one time. Looking forward, that sectional division is one of the key things, from a state level, that we should look at. Virginia is one of the few states that has a tiny, tiny Republican influence because Virginia goes all the way up to Wheeling, and there are a couple of Republican newspapers up there. That sectional division is key if you look at it just from a state level.

ED AYERS   The title of this session is "Predictions for the Election of 1860." What do people think is going to happen?

JEAN BAKER   You could only answer that regionally at this point, or sectionally I should say. That's the real point. There is this middle group of states that are, I think, uncertain and that really are interested in the possibilities of, not necessarily a third nation, but a border-state confederacy to broker peace between the North and South. Kentucky, Missouri, Delaware, Maryland—Virginia is the big player. John Pendleton Kennedy, a writer in Maryland, produces a pamphlet and goes around this area trying to set up a confederation to be an independent broker between the North and South. This is the only possibility: folks in the South who vote are going to vote Democratic, folks in the North are going to vote Republican.

I want to say one other thing. There is a group of Americans who don't vote. This is a time in our history where the percentages of turnouts are over 65 percent. Nonetheless, even at 70 and 75 percent, there's a whole group of Americans that, as today, just simply aren't caught up in what we've been talking about.

DAN CROFTS   Let's just say quickly here that if Republicans win Indiana, Illinois, and Pennsylvania, they're in a position to elect the president. In the 1858 elections, they did very well in Pennsylvania. They're knocking on the door in Indiana and Illinois. And that's the name of the game.

ED AYERS   Do they have an idea that Abraham Lincoln might be their nominee by December 31?

JEAN BAKER   I think Abraham Lincoln has that idea.

NELSON LANKFORD   Seward is still the favorite.

ED AYERS   So it is not clear that Abraham Lincoln is going to be nominated for the Republican Party?

LIZ VARON   It's not clear, but he has his partisans in the West. He's laying low. He's thinking about it, but he doesn't want to come out and be fired at and shot down too early. He's trying to get his name in the news, particularly in the western newspapers, Chicago and so on, by giving speeches in the midwestern states. The eastern party elite doesn't yet see him as the man.

DAN CROFTS   Oddsmakers wouldn't give Lincoln very good chances of being nominated.

NELSON LANKFORD   But even though they don't know who the Republican nominee is, many people in the Deep South say, "If any Republican, whoever they nominate, is elected, we're out of here." That terrifies people in the Upper South, and sets up a tension, even before this later thing, between the Lower South and the Upper South.

LIZ VARON   It should be noted that the fear of a Republican election is two seemingly contradictory fears. One is this fear of invasion, and there had been language of invasion in the air and in the political atmosphere since Kansas and Nebraska. But there is a second fear, and that is a fear of infiltration—that the Republicans would use patronage and persuasion to peel away those non-slaveholding yeomen and bring them into the Republican ranks. It doesn't make a lot of sense to juxtapose those two fears, but slavery's defenders oftentimes made opportunistic arguments. Here was the argument that the Republicans might succeed, particularly in the Upper South, in peeling away some of those non-slaveholders.

ED AYERS   To sum up: Immigration matters a lot, economic development matters a lot, the spread of new communications and transportation matters a lot, population expansion matters a lot, international relations and imagining the different boundaries of the United States is at play. The political system has gone through enormous changes. It's hard for us to imagine it just being ripped apart—parties that have been around for generations disappearing and all these kinds of things. We need to understand all these layers if we're going to understand the Civil War.

Second Question-and-Answer Session

for "Making Sense of John Brown's Raid"
and "Predictions for the Election of 1860"

Participants in the question-and-answer session were Jean Baker, David Blight, Daniel Crofts, Nelson Lankford, David Reynolds, Manisha Sinha, Elizabeth Varon, and Clarence Walker, with Edward L. Ayers moderating.

ED AYERS   The questions that have poured in are the big ones, not so much just about the events, but about the larger context of those events. The first one is from Kim O'Connell: "With the newspapers in 1859, was there a paper that was known for its reporting? Was unbiased reporting valued or were publications more about propaganda?" We've been talking a lot about newspapers. We can see how they've been used in Kansas-Nebraska in many ways, even in Dred Scott, or certainly Anthony Burns. The things we've been talking about take on real importance by being spread in the media. Was there a place that people could turn to get what we consider today an unbiased report?

JEAN BAKER   No. I think the thing about these newspapers is that often the editors are running for political office. So if you want to get elected, you begin your newspaper and hope that someone in your party will buy it. And of course, you're not going to be a nonpartisan when it comes to your own election.

LIZ VARON   But there is a distinction. Some newspapers are simply borrowing while some are actually reporting and generating news. The richer ones like the *New York Tribune* of Horace Greeley could hire people on the scene, say, in Kansas or send reporters to places like Kansas to generate stories. And they did so. It's not that you were getting unbiased news, but you were getting it its first time through the system. Other papers would borrow from those papers that could hire correspondents or send them into the field.

DAVID REYNOLDS The most popular national newspaper was the *New York Herald*, which was definitely proslavery and pro-Democratic. The *Tribune* was Republican, antislavery. But they were slanted.

DAN CROFTS The national media are beginning to coalesce in New York City. We just mentioned the *Herald* and the *Tribune*; if there is something that's a little bit down the middle, it's the *New York Times* of all things, which is moderate Republican and not going out of its way to stigmatize Southerners. It is actually supporting a Democratic candidate for mayor in the fall of '59 to differentiate itself from the hard-line Republican *New York Tribune.*

DAVID REYNOLDS It's not today's *New York Times,* which is such a preeminent newspaper. Back then it had just begun.

DAVID BLIGHT Newspaper editors were public figures. Horace Greeley's speaking tours were national phenomena.

NELSON LANKFORD You could find opposing views if you looked because papers were like magpies, borrowing from one another in different parts of the country. They would just reprint articles from a paper of opposing opinions. They reprinted word for word. They needed to fill up their space. If you wanted to look, you could find different opinions, even during the Civil War.

ED AYERS Why would they print opposing opinions in their own newspapers?

NELSON LANKFORD They weren't reprinting to reprint the opposing opinions. The opinion that they quoted from an opposing paper wasn't an editorial, necessarily, but a news report that had political material embedded in it.

DAVID REYNOLDS The abolitionist *Liberator* of Boston would print extensive proslavery articles because they were so patently false. They conveyed, "Oh, look how silly the *New Orleans Picayune* is." They wouldn't even have to preface it. They would just print it. The same thing happened down South. They'd reprint John Brown's speeches because obviously they were so ridiculous. Everybody knew that they were silly. That was the understanding.

MANISHA SINHA The *Liberator* would publish Southern newspaper articles under the heading "Refuge of Oppression." We talked a lot about the Northern newspapers, and it's true that all the newspapers were very partisan and the editors were partisan. They were either running for office or supporting people running for office. But we need to talk a little about the Southern newspapers, I think. Even though they were partisan, everyone knew that the *Charleston Mercury* was this fire-eating secessionist newspaper, while the *Richmond Enquirer,* which was a Democratic proslavery newspaper, could still be relied on, at times, to take a middle-of-the-road unionist position. And its opposing paper, the *Richmond Whig,* too.

ED AYERS　So how could people possibly know what to believe? I mean, to answer the question, was there anywhere to go for an unbiased reporting of what was happening?

MANISHA SINHA　What is so interesting about these newspapers is that they would, many times, reprint entire speeches being said in Congress. If you wanted to read a speech that was not put out in a pamphlet, you could go to any of these newspapers and read the entire proceedings of Congress. Sometimes they would have proceedings of trials, important trials like John Brown's trial, and they would just simply reprint it. For a lot of the cases involving the reopening of the African slave trade, when there were some instances of illegal importation, the most valuable sources come from antebellum newspapers that simply reprinted the entire proceeding of the court, which we otherwise cannot get now because during the Civil War many of these courthouses and their records were burned.

ED AYERS　So if people could avoid the editorials, there were some of the raw materials for these instances. I do think it's worth reiterating in response to Kim's question that the media as we think of them today did not exist. You had the power to reach and persuade and caricature, but not really the power to offer an objective interpretation.

　A question that three different people asked is one that I think all of us who talk about the Civil War and what may become the Civil War ask ourselves: How prominent was the concept of states' rights among Americans in 1859? We've heard a lot about slavery, but was this the primary impetus to the coming crisis?

DAVID BLIGHT　One of them.

JEAN BAKER　Primary one.

DAVID BLIGHT　It's a very, very important one. The question of federalism, the nature of federalism, the nature of state/federal relationships is as old as the Constitution, if not older. But in any instance of the use of states' rights, and it was employed by Northerners just as much as by Southerners before the American Civil War, as all of us know, one always has to ask, states' rights for what? The significance of states' rights—states' rights doctrine, a use of states' rights language—is always in the issue to which it's applied. That issue might have been the Hartford Convention of 1814, convened by a bunch of New Englanders for economic reasons and trade reasons. That issue might have been a bunch of abolitionists in Wisconsin creating personal liberty laws to protect fugitive slaves, or it might have been secessionists, talking about secession that might happen later. So yes, states' rights was very, very important in this debate. But for any use of states' rights, the significance is the issue to which it gets applied, not just the doctrine itself, in my view.

NELSON LANKFORD   Henry Wise, the Virginia governor, gave a speech in which he said, "I'm willing to fight for states' rights and the rights of slavery." States' rights and the rights of slavery. He could not tease them apart by the late 1850s, early 1860s. They were part and parcel to him of the same thing.

ED AYERS   So are historians of our time so obsessed with slavery that we have lost sight of some important constitutional and economic issues?

MANISHA SINHA   I do think that the question of states' rights was not insignificant; but it was, as the previous panelists have said, very linked to the issue of slavery, at least in the antebellum period. If you trace the history of states' rights, and you go back to the Kentucky-Virginia Resolutions of 1798, at that time it seemed to be linked with the issue of civil liberties and local democracy against the Alien and Sedition Acts of the Adams administration. What happens in the 1830s with the Nullification Crisis is that the South Carolinians—and this is where the South Carolinians have, I guess, a lead on Virginians—led by John C. Calhoun, very clearly connect the issue of states' rights with the defense of slavery. It's a question of opposing federal laws on tariff, and an anticipated law on emancipation.

That intertwining of the defense of slavery and states' rights clearly continues right down to the antebellum period when they come up with this notion of state sovereignty that goes even beyond states' rights, which would then allow a state to secede from the Union because states are the true sovereign entities, rather than Madison's original conception of states' rights as divided sovereignty between the federal government and the state governments.

As the need to defend slavery becomes more urgent, Southerners articulate an even more extreme version of states' rights, coming up with this conception of sovereignty and secession. Now, it's true, as David Blight pointed out, that in the 1850s Northerners opposing the Fugitive Slave Law start evoking states' rights. But it's really linked with the Southern constitutional tradition. And interestingly enough, on the eve of the Civil War, Southerners always evoke the Constitution, a strict interpretation of the Constitution, states' rights; and Northerners like Lincoln always talk about the Declaration of Independence.

LIZ VARON   There's also a strong cult of state honor both in the North and in the South. When Northerners are, for example, speaking out against the Fugitive Slave Act, they often speak in defense of the honor of their states. In the Anthony Burns case, the honor of Massachusetts has been besmirched by the efforts of slave catchers to send him back into slavery. We can't downplay how strong state identification and a sense of state pride and honor were in the North as well as in the South.

ED AYERS   That raises another question that people sometimes point to as a reason for the sectional conflict: the difference in cultures between the North and the South.

CLARENCE WALKER   It seems to me what separates the North from the South is really the institution of slavery. Southerners spoke English as Northerners did, they worshipped in similar churches, they intermarried. There was trade and commerce between the two sections. If there is a distinction between the two sections, it is that one is based on free labor and the other is based on slavery. Slavery sits at the heart of this great divide. This notion of two civilizations is a question that historians have been arguing for a long time.

DAVID REYNOLDS   In 1861 the vice president of the Confederacy, Alexander Stephens, says that the great cornerstone of the Confederacy is slavery. This is the first civilization based on, as he called it, the inferiority of the Negro, that it's a great moral truth and is what we are based on. On the other hand, at the same time, the South had a real sense of cultural difference. It thought of the North as being full of "-isms," competing -isms: Women's rights, spiritualism, mesmerism, magnetism, abolitionism.

ED AYERS   And it was.

DAVID REYNOLDS   It was a chaotic society, unstable, just going nuts. And the South was very stable. It had the slaves down here, it had the masters up here, it had the Episcopal Church, which was very popular down in the South. Everything was stable and orderly. The North was full of anarchists, and that's where the Mormons had begun in the Burned-Over District.

LIZ VARON   It was cultural, but there was a gnawing sense of cultural inferiority on the part of the South. There was a defense of Southern stability, but Republicans like to say that wherever the Republican Party is strong, you have printing presses and churches and schools and journals and all the signs of cultural refinement. Those things are lacking in the South. Southerners heard this, and there was a real sense of wounded pride over this charge of cultural inferiority, and also some worry that there was some truth to it.

DAN CROFTS   The Northern free-labor ideology that the Republican Party hijacks is a kind of idealized version of how things are going in the North—that this is a society where people can get ahead through hard work and enterprise and playing by the rules. It's the wave of the future, and we expect that the more sensible people in the South will come around and realize that this would be better for them, too.

ED AYERS   Because they are hardworking farmers just like we are, right? And it goes back to Liz's point earlier about the Southern fear of infiltration by the Republicans, because Southerners are hardworking, dedicated people who are trying to build their farms and families themselves. The Republicans thought this would be a language that would actually cut across any other differences. It might have worked if you had not had the war.

CLARENCE WALKER   Southerners believed in free labor, too; they just didn't believe in it for black folks. Free labor was a universal in bourgeois culture of the nineteenth-century United States. Just in the minds of Southerners, it could not be applied to black people.

MANISHA SINHA   I think when Northerners talked about free labor, they did not mean wage work. They thought of wage work as a stepping stone toward independent proprietorship of a farm or artisanal shop. They did not see it as a permanent condition. Of course, that was an idealized version, as has been mentioned. But I think it's also important to remember that Southerners called the Republican Party the Brown-Helper party. By that they were referring to Hinton Rowan Helper, a Southern non-slaveholder who had indicted slavery on economic grounds. He was from North Carolina. There was this real fear that the Republican Party would appeal to the so-called lower classes in the South, non-slaveholding whites, slaves, free blacks, and create a sort of fifth column in the South.

ED AYERS   It goes back to Dan's point about that idealized version of the North. We've seen that the South is actually *not* "not prosperous." The South is actually richer per capita than the white North.

DAVID BLIGHT   It's why white Southerners are so threatened by this Republican Party. One of the most ubiquitous terms in 1859 was this idea of abolition emissaries. And lo and behold, what does John Brown do but become the ultimate abolition emissary of all time. There had been all kinds of rumors of slave insurrection in the late 1850s, especially in election years. I think David Reynolds made a very good point about these real cultural differences. One of those great cultural differences between North and South populations we cannot escape is that we do have different conceptions of what social or historical change will be. The South is a hierarchal, organic, ordered society, where change, if it ever happens, is going to come over a long term, slowly, and you might not even notice it. Whereas in the North, it's expanding. Tocqueville captured this in his book (that's a book we've all read in 1859). These Northerners are always moving. They move to build a house, and move again before they put a roof on it, and so on. To Southerners this was an unordered world, and they had to resist it.

DAVID REYNOLDS   One reason why Lincoln wins in 1860 is that he distances himself very much from abolitionism, from the Northern fanaticism, from the reform movements. He positions himself in such a way that he can appeal to certain people that might be wavering between the North and the South. He denounces John Brown, he's anti-abolition—and that's one reason he inches in and wins over enough people.

JEAN BAKER That's why William Henry Seward, who we all would think would have been nominated, is not nominated. He's too radical.

ED AYERS He's too much like the way we're saying the North is to be elected in the North.

JEAN BAKER On the other hand, there is a position beyond which Abraham Lincoln will not move. And that, of course, is what gets us even beyond 1860.

ED AYERS Two questions from Bill Brockner and John Zervot: "Why didn't compromise work? Somebody pointed out earlier that this has been the great American tradition. Was there something wrong with the American system? Did all these different vectors just happened to intersect and bring on something, or was this a failure of American politics and government?"

CLARENCE WALKER I don't know if it was a failure of American politics, but it seems to be that the political system, as it was constructed at the end of the eighteenth century, was constructed to negotiate issues in a way that slavery really contradicted. This was a moral question. You have two deeply religious sections here, and after a period of time the dialectic is produced in which they come to see the other side as evil. And Christians do not compromise with evil. Compromise has failed in 1820. It fails again in 1850, and by 1860, 1861, what is there left to compromise? The South, I think, feels it has nothing left to compromise with the North. It has affirmed the positive nature of slavery.

DAN CROFTS The difficulty is the Republicans had won the presidential election in 1860 clean and clear. There was no question that they had assembled the majority of electoral votes. They were not about to fritter that away.

ED AYERS There was nothing to compromise about.

DAVID BLIGHT There still was . . . in the late 1850s. One way to think about it—this isn't the only answer, but one way to think about it—is that the Dred Scott case ruined moderation. It ruined what was left of compromise because you think there is a structural failure here. The first American republic, folks, is failing. It failed. Dred Scott is a Supreme Court decision. The Supreme Court finally weighs in on this decades-old controversy and what does it say? It says Calhoun and the South have been right all along. Northerners who have built a political movement, a persuasion around this idea that, above all else, they will stop the expansion of slavery are now told, "You can't do that." Where is the moderation? Where's the position after Dred Scott that can actually be compromised?

MANISHA SINHA   There were compromises proposed, mainly from the state of Virginia. There were people from Virginia who were pushing very hard for a compromise over the issue of slavery. What they were asking the Republicans to do was basically to forsake the electoral platform, which was non-extension of slavery. That was one position that Lincoln refused to compromise on. And then if we go further down the road, and you have the Compromise of 1877, and it inaugurates a racial nightmare in the South in terms of Jim Crow and sharecropping, you wonder whether we should be valorizing compromises to the extent that we do in American political history.

LIZ VARON   You can also note about compromise that in some sense the quintessential compromise position, a belief in the gradual dismantling of slavery—gradualism, the alternative to abolitionism—dies a hard death. Secession doesn't put to rest the fantasies that some voluntary, compensated, gradual solution will solve this. Lincoln and the Republicans continue to push for such a thing, and slaveholders refuse again and again and again and again to accept that offer. So that dies a very hard death.

DAN CROFTS   It's worth mentioning that Lincoln, in his inaugural address, March 4, 1861, promises to accept a constitutional amendment that had passed Congress the night before, forever protecting slavery in the states where it already existed.

DAVID BLIGHT   The original Thirteenth Amendment.

NELSON LANKFORD   If compromise had been successful, as all those people, especially in the Upper South, had wanted, if they had come to some kind of compromise, the problem that we have looking back on it is, would it have then condemned one more generation to slavery? How many more, two? We don't know. That's one problem we have looking back on it and judging what such a compromise would have been like.

Closing Remarks

EDWARD L. AYERS   In some ways we're left at the end of 1859 still trying to explain how a war that no one wanted, that brought a result that no one anticipated, happened. That's still where we are. What we're better prepared to understand now is how that could be. We can't wall off any facet of human experience if we're talking about this issue. It includes everything from gender and racial identity to demography to economic change to political change. I think the important thing we've seen is how rich American history is, how deep these challenges are, how many people of goodwill and deep dedication we have exploring this issue, how much there is still to learn and understand about this period of American history.

If we take nothing else from this, we take the idea that the history we're living ourselves right now is a lot more interesting and complicated than the versions that we tend to get and the slogans that we tend to throw around. I'd like to think that the lesson of 1859 is to encourage a certain level of humility in the face of the history that we're living ourselves in an effort to try to understand beyond just today's headline, to think about what major forces are moving us, what things are pulling on us that we may not even feel, to understand that deeply entrenched problems simply will not go away just because we want them to. I think these are things that our panelists have helped us understand, and it's been a tremendous honor for the University of Richmond to have a chance to participate in this great conversation.

Conclusion

Marking the Civil War Sesquicentennial–
Will We Do Better This Time?

David W. Blight

David W. Blight, a participant in the conference, was asked to write a review for the Chronicle of Higher Education. *The following appeared in the May 26, 2009, issue.*

In 1961–65 the centennial commemoration of the Civil War was a political and historical debacle. Fraught, to say the least, by cold war nationalism, racism among its leadership as well as the general populace, an enduring hold of the Lost Cause on popular imagination, and a country violently divided by the civil rights movement, the official Civil War centennial refused to face the challenge of causes and consequences. Instead, a reconciliationist, Blue-Gray celebration of soldiers' valor and re-emergent national greatness forged out of conflict dominated the scene. After a hundred years, North and South had managed a long, complex reconciliation rooted in a master narrative of mutual heroism in a war in which everyone had fought for their sense of the "right." But the national reunion of the sections had been purchased by the Jim Crow system and a racially segregated, tragically stunted national memory.

Now fast forward to the kickoff of a commemoration of the sesquicentennial. Jumbotrons in basketball arenas and panels of academic historians are not normally associated with each other. But an event held at the University of Richmond recently, "America on the Eve of the Civil War," was anything but normal. Planned and moderated by Edward L. Ayers, president of the university and a distinguished historian of the South and the Civil War, the all-day symposium, with sixteen of us, historians, on panels of four each, attracted an extraordinary audience of some two thousand people from Virginia and twenty-six other states. It was the first of seven annual events planned by the Virginia Sesquicentennial of the American Civil War Commission. No state suffered more loss and devastation than Virginia during the Civil War, and nowhere have people remembered that conflict with as much reverence and controversy. The Virginia commission opted to begin the sesquicentennial early to stress the theme of the war's causation.

What would bring so many people on a weekday to listen to historians reflect on why the United States collapsed into disunion in the late 1850s? First, the symposium drew its energy and vision from Ayers himself. An advocate of what he calls "deep contingency" (keeping our understanding of history within its own changing context), Ayers instructed all panelists to focus on the year 1859 and to discuss nothing that happened after that year. We were to be in that time, of its conditions and circumstances, not yet aware of the impending secession crisis and war. By and large that approach worked, as Ayers posed questions and the historians delved into details and debated the political and economic situation on the ground. The novel approach prevented us from quoting or referring to other scholars, which is our habit. It also led to some awkwardness as many panelists jokingly spoke of "the great events to come which will go unmentioned."

A second reason for the popularity of the symposium is simply that the Civil War still attracts legions of "buffs," a term that is sometimes far too dismissive and encompasses serious readers, collectors, reenactors, battlefield preservationists, and educators at all levels. With the sesquicentennial looming in 2011–15, we are likely to experience a flood of attention to the Civil War era from film and publishing, tourism and school curricula, and possibly even American political culture.

But a third, and perhaps the most important, reason for the turnout in Richmond may be that in recent decades powerful new winds have been blowing through Civil War history, from the academy to the furthest reaches of public memory. Revolutions in social, African American, and women's history, as well as the advent of new modes of military history—treating the war from the perspectives of common soldiers, homefronts as well as battlefronts, slaves and captive prisoners as well as generals and strategy—have transformed a field once seemingly dominated by the "view from headquarters" or the valor of the Blue and the

Gray. An increasing number of historians, moreover, have written about the memory of the Civil War in American culture as one of the most dominant elements of an ever-changing American national identity and as a driving force in the history of race relations. And most significant, these new winds have been felt deeply and widely in public history forums. It is not your father's or your grandmother's Civil War history anymore, even—and especially—in the South.

Or is it? We shall see.

The Lost Cause tradition—as both a version of history and as a racial ideology—is certainly still very much alive in neo-Confederate organizations, on numerous Web sites, among white supremacist groups, in staunch advocates of the Confederate battle flag, and even among some mainstream American politicians. Multitudes still cannot bring themselves to confront the story of slavery as both lived experience and the central cause of the Civil War.

But countless others have done so, often overcoming the essence of their early education or family lore. Above all, the greatest challenge for academic historians of this pivotal era has been to persuade the interested public, including some politicians and public historians (those who work in museums and at historic sites), that the causes and consequences of the Civil War are easily as important as the drama of the third day at the battle of Gettysburg. In other words, the deepest answers to why that terrible war occurred, and why we have struggled as a people to face and solve its eternal legacies, may have more lasting meaning than the heartfelt pathos one feels standing today on the "sacred ground" of one of its beautiful battlefields.

Such was the tenor and purpose of the Richmond symposium. We were there to understand the society, South and North, the political and economic systems, the ideologically driven defenders of slavery as well as its fierce opponents, and especially the lives of ordinary people (white and black, free and enslaved, slave owning and not, bankers and dirt farmers) living at a time when their country teetered on the edge of the abyss of fratricidal war. The conference opened with welcoming remarks by Ayers, who urged everyone to look back at the Civil War era with "fresh eyes," but also made it clear he was thrilled this could happen in the "former capital of the Confederacy." When William J. Howell, the Republican Speaker of the House of Delegates in Virginia and chairman of the state's sesquicentennial commission, announced openly that this anniversary season would focus on the "causes" and "enduring legacies" of the conflict, I had to pinch myself and drop my cynical guard, realizing that fifty years earlier such a remark would never have been uttered by the leader of a Southern state legislature. This was not to be a remembrance of the Lost Cause. Then Governor Tim Kaine, a Democrat, addressed us and demanded that this time the Civil War must be treated with "analysis and commemoration" and that the events of 1861–65 were "not in the past at all," but alive in our present every day. Analysis? Bravo, I said, under my breath.

And so the analysis commenced, with panels entitled "Taking Stock of the Nation in 1859," "The Future of Virginia and the South," "Making Sense of John Brown's Raid," and finally, "Predictions for the Election of 1860." Only rarely did panelists veer off into arcane subjects; Ayers kept us on course. In most cases, the audience was spared the certainty of well-honed interpretations in favor of open discussion of the unsettled and huge character of American expansion in the 1850s, of that era's swirling issues of immigration and anti-Catholicism, of a transportation and communication revolution that boggled the imagination of its time even more than the Internet does in our age. And I suspect many were stunned at what they learned of the scale of the domestic slave trade, in Richmond's own streets and across the South. (One recent study concludes that in 1859–60 the value of slaves sold in the domestic market was $9.56 million, many millions more in today's dollars.)

As it turns out, we had to admit that Americans of the late 1850s were as confused, excited, and frightened about their futures as people in any other era. Their politics consisted of a raucous, transforming party system, quickly dividing over the slavery question and thriving on huge voter turnout. Virginia had a booming and diverse economy, despite growing very little cotton and exporting to the Deep South ever-increasing numbers of slaves, the nation's single largest financial asset. A couple of the panelists in the John Brown session waxed somewhat romantic in their defense of the radical abolitionist, stimulating a useful exchange about what constitutes justifiable revolutionary violence.

The rise of that relatively unknown lawyer from Illinois to the presidency in 1860 was imagined only by a few midwestern political managers at the end of 1859. As our historian-pundits handicapped the impending election with both deep knowledge and a sense of wonder, most suggested William H. Seward as the likely candidate of the new Republican Party. And slavery and race certainly seemed to be tearing the nation apart, while not everyone thought about those issues every day. The past, much less the future, most of us historians concluded, is an unstable story even when we know a great deal about it. Back in the green room and over lunch, we chuckled over our strange roles as near occupants of an actual 1859, but out on stage displayed our humbled expertise.

Audience members submitted hundreds of questions through the course of the day that were processed by graduate students. Ayers has kindly provided me with the full list of questions, including many submitted online from the webcast audience. As a whole, the queries reflect an informed audience eager to know more. Many asked about the anomalous situation of free blacks in the South, and several were fascinated by John Brown and violence. Even more pushed for a longer discussion of "states' rights" as a cause of America's predicament in the 1850s. In a Q&A after one of the panels, we confronted the issue of states' rights, most of us trying to demonstrate that the significance of the doctrine is always in the cause for which it is employed, whether by Northerners or Southerners in antebellum America or by judges and politicians today. The relationship of states' rights to slavery in all discussions of Civil War causation appears to be an eternal riddle in American public memory. Federalism and "state sovereignty," as Southerners tended to call it, demand an understanding beyond slogans and uses that often skirt the deeper issues at stake in the 1850s—slavery, race, and the future of labor in an expanding republic. The sheer range of audience questions indicated a serious desire to stop, take stock, and comprehend why that war came about when it did.

If the self-selected audience can be any kind of model, and if the Richmond event can be even modestly duplicated elsewhere, the sesquicentennial will be very different from the fiasco of the centennial of the Civil War in 1961–65 (a story detailed in the excellent book by Robert J. Cook, *Troubled Commemoration,* published by Louisiana State University Press in 2007). General Ulysses S. Grant III, retired, chairman of the federal centennial commission, declared his "close feeling" for the Civil War in 1960 as though it were a family inheritance. "The war did not divide us," he announced. "Rather, it united us, in spite of a long period of bitterness, and made us the greatest and most powerful nation the world had ever seen." To Grant, the centennial provided a nationalistic celebration among white people, full of "colorful ceremonies . . . exhibitions of war trophies," and plenty of "memorials, parades, and new historical markers."

Such language would have been utterly out of place at the Richmond sesquicentennial opening in April. But we should approach this anniversary and its myriad events with caution born of the past. We are living in a new era, inspired by the election of an African American president and by widely disseminated new understandings of the causes and consequences of the Civil War. But how wide? We do not fully know.

The Lost Cause still endures in the twenty-first century because it serves many sentimental and racial desires in the present. And I suspect that if we could conduct a national referendum on why and how Americans want their Civil War history and memory served up, the majority would still opt for the military drama, for the narrative of battles and leaders. We still need that history too, but this time the story ought to be as much about emancipation as it is about Robert E. Lee's daring invasions of the North or Ulysses S. Grant's determination in the Wilderness Campaign. This time, we need events and publications with mass appeal that will explain not only the complex causes of the war, but its legacies as well.

In his "I Have a Dream" speech at the Lincoln Memorial in 1963, in the midst of the centennial, Martin Luther King Jr. took his time getting to the "dream" metaphor. The central metaphor of the beginning of that speech was the "promissory note" that had come back labeled "insufficient funds" in the "bank of American justice." One hundred years after emancipation, said King so memorably, "the Negro is not free." Last November 4, as Barack Obama strode onto the stage in Grant Park in Chicago, something in excess of 50 percent of the people all over America were cheering or weeping uncontrollably. In his speech that night, Obama declared his political lineage by invoking King as well as Lincoln. The next morning in the *New York Times,* the columnist Thomas Friedman declared November 4 the day the Civil War ended in America. As the sesquicentennial nears, we are likely to witness the foolishness of Friedman's exuberant claim. With jobless numbers soaring and the poverty rate among all children predicted to reach 27 percent in the next year—and among African American children, a frightening 50 percent—we should declare nothing truly ended in our history.

Legacies can take endless forms—physical, political, literary, emotional. This time, we must commemorate our Civil War in all its meanings, but above all we must commemorate and understand emancipation as its most enduring challenge. This time, the fighting of the Civil War itself should not unite us in pathos and nostalgia alone; but maybe, just maybe, we will give ourselves the chance to find unity in a shared history of conflict, in a genuine sense of tragedy, and in a conflicted memory stared squarely in the face.

Conference Participants

EDWARD L. AYERS, Conference Chair, is President of the University of Richmond and Professor of History. Prior to 2007, he was Dean of Arts and Sciences at the University of Virginia, where he began his teaching career in 1980. Ayers was named the National Professor of the Year by the Carnegie Foundation for the Advancement of Teaching in 2003. A historian of the American South, Ayers has written and edited ten books. *The Promise of the New South: Life After Reconstruction* (1992) was a finalist for both the National Book Award and the Pulitzer Prize. *In the Presence of Mine Enemies: Civil War in the Heart of America* (2003) won the Bancroft Prize for distinguished writing in American history and the Beveridge Prize for the best book in English on the history of the Americas since 1492. A pioneer in digital history, Ayers created *The Valley of the Shadow: Two Communities in the American Civil War,* a Web site that has attracted millions of users and won major prizes in the teaching of history. He received his BA from the University of Tennessee and his MA and PhD from Yale University.

DR. JEAN H. BAKER is Professor of History at Goucher College, where she has taught since 1972. She received her BA from Goucher and her MA and PhD from Johns Hopkins University and is the author of ten books, including *Mary Todd Lincoln: A Biography* (1987) and the recently published *Sisters: The Lives of America's Suffragists* (2005).

DR. DAVID W. BLIGHT is the Class of 1954 Professor of American History at Yale University. He is Director of the Gilder Lehrman Center for the Study of Slavery, Resistance, and Abolition at Yale. His book, *Race and Reunion: The Civil War in American Memory* (2001), received eight awards, including the Bancroft Prize, the Abraham Lincoln Prize, and the Frederick Douglass Prize, as well as four awards from the Organization of American Historians. He is the author of four books; the editor and coeditor of six and four volumes, respectively; and a frequent book reviewer for the *Washington Post Book World,* the *Chicago Tribune,* and other newspapers. He received his undergraduate degree from Michigan State University and his PhD from the University of Wisconsin–Madison.

MS. CHRISTY S. COLEMAN is President of the American Civil War Center at Historic Tredegar. From 1999 to 2005 she served as President and CEO of the Charles H. Wright Museum of African American History in Detroit, the largest African American museum in the United States. Her work as a consultant includes the Smithsonian Institution, Monticello, Mount Vernon, and the National Underground Railroad Freedom Center. Ms. Coleman received her BA and MA from Hampton University.

DR. DANIEL W. CROFTS has taught at The College of New Jersey since 1975. He received his BA from Wabash College and MA and PhD from Yale University. His principal books are *Reluctant Confederates: Upper South Unionists in the Secession Crisis* (1989) and *Old Southampton: Politics and Society in a Virginia County, 1834–1869* (1992). His new book, *A Secession Crisis Enigma: William Henry Hurlbert and "The Diary of a Public Man,"* will be published in 2010.

DR. CHARLES B. DEW teaches the history of the South and the Civil War and Reconstruction at Williams College, where he is Ephraim Williams Professor of American History. He is a graduate of Williams College and completed his PhD at the Johns Hopkins University. He is the author of three books: *Ironmaker to the Confederacy: Joseph R. Anderson and the Tredegar Iron Works* (1999); *Bond of Iron: Master and Slave at Buffalo Forge* (1994); and *Apostles of Disunion: Southern Secession Commissioners and the Causes of the Civil War* (2001). *Ironmaker to the Confederacy* and *Apostles of Disunion* each received the Fletcher Pratt

Award, given by the Civil War Roundtable of New York for the best nonfiction book on the Civil War in its year of publication. *Bond of Iron* was awarded the Organization of American Historians' Elliott Rudwick Prize and was a finalist for the Lincoln Prize.

DR. GARY W. GALLAGHER is the John L. Nau III Professor in the History of the American Civil War at the University of Virginia. He is a graduate of Adams State College in Colorado and earned his MA and PhD in history from the University of Texas at Austin. He is the author, coauthor, or editor of more than thirty books, among them *Causes Won, Lost, and Forgotten: How Hollywood and Popular Art Shape What We Know about the Civil War* (2008); *Lee and His Generals in War and Memory* (1998); and *The Confederate War* (1997). He edits two book series at the University of North Carolina Press, "Civil War America" and "Military Campaigns of the Civil War," and is a recipient of the Lincoln Prize and the Fletcher Pratt Award

DR. WALTER JOHNSON is the Winthrop Professor of History and Professor of African American Studies at Harvard University. His first book, *Soul by Soul: Life Inside the Antebellum Slave Market* (1999), was an interdisciplinary study of slavery that brought together cultural, economic, and political history and shifted the historical focus of slavery from the plantation to the marketplace. *Soul by Soul* won the John Hope Franklin Prize, the Avery O. Craven Prize, and the Thomas J. Wilson Prize. Walter Johnson received his BA from Amherst College and PhD from Princeton University.

DR. ROBERT C. KENZER is the William Binford Vest Chair in History and American Studies at the University of Richmond. He teaches courses on the Civil War Era, the Civil War in Film and Literature, and Abraham Lincoln. He received his BA in History from the University of California at Santa Barbara and MA and PhD from Harvard University. He is the author of *Kinship and Neighborhood in a Southern Community: Orange County, North Carolina, 1849–1881* (1987) and *Enterprising Southerners: Black Economic Success in North Carolina, 1865–1915* (1997) and the coeditor of *Enemies of My Country: New Perspectives on Unionists in the Civil War South* (2001).

DR. GREGG D. KIMBALL is Director of Publications and Educational Services at the Library of Virginia. He holds a PhD in history from the University of Virginia and an MLS from the University of Maryland. His publications include *American City, Southern Place: A Cultural History of Antebellum Richmond* (2000).

DR. NELSON D. LANKFORD is the editor of the *Virginia Magazine of History and Biography,* the quarterly journal of the Virginia Historical Society. His other publications include *Cry Havoc! The Crooked Road to Civil War, 1861* (2007); *Richmond Burning: The Last Days of the Confederate Capital* (2002); and *Eye of the Storm: A Civil War Odyssey* (co-edited with Charles F. Bryan Jr., 2000). He received his undergraduate degree from the University of Richmond and his MBA and PhD from Indiana University, Bloomington.

DR. LAURANETT L. LEE is the founding curator of African American history at the Virginia Historical Society. She received a BA in communications from Mundelein College, an MA in American history from Virginia State University, and a PhD in American history from the University of Virginia. She is the author of *Making the American Dream Work: A Cultural History of African Americans in Hopewell, Virginia* (2008).

DR. DAVID S. REYNOLDS is Distinguished Professor of English and American Studies at the Graduate Center of the City University of New York. He is the author of *Waking Giant: America in the Age of Jackson* (2008) and *John Brown, Abolitionist: The Man Who Killed Slavery, Sparked the Civil War, and Seeded Civil Rights* (2005). He received a BA magna cum laude from Amherst College and a PhD from the University of California, Berkeley.

DR. MANISHA SINHA is Associate Professor of Afro-American Studies and History at the University of Massachusetts, Amherst. She received her doctorate from Columbia University, where her dissertation was nominated for the Bancroft prize. She is the author of *The Counterrevolution of Slavery: Politics and Ideology in Antebellum South Carolina* (2000); coeditor of *African American Mosaic: A Documentary History* *from the Slave Trade to the Twenty First Century* (2 vols., 2004) and *Contested Democracy: Freedom, Race and Power in American History* (2007); and editor of the "Race and the Atlantic World, 1700–1900" series of the University of Georgia Press.

DR. ELIZABETH R. VARON is Professor of History at Temple University and Associate Director of the Center for the Humanities at Temple. She received her MA from Swarthmore College and PhD from Yale. Her books include *We Mean to be Counted: White Women and Politics in Antebellum Virginia* (1998), winner of the Lerner-Scott Prize of the American Historical Association; *Southern Lady, Yankee Spy: The True Story of Elizabeth Van Lew, A Union Agent in the Heart of the Confederacy* (2003), winner of the Lillian Smith Prize of the Southern Regional Council; and *Disunion! The Coming of the American Civil War, 1789–1859,* volume 1 of the Littlefield History of the Civil War Era series (2008).

DR. CLARENCE E. WALKER is Professor of History and Cultural Studies at the University of California, Davis. He is the author of *A Rock in a Weary Land: The African Methodist Episcopal Church During the Civil War and Reconstruction* (1982); *Deromanticizing Black History: Critical Essays and Reappraisals* (1991); *We Can't Go Home Again: An Argument About Afrocentrism* (2001); and *Mongrel Nation: The America Begotten By Thomas Jefferson and Sally Hemings* (2009); and the coauthor (with Gregory D. Smithers) of *The Preacher and the Politician: Jeremiah Wright, Barack Obama, and Race in America* (2009). He received his BA from California State University, San Francisco, and his MA and PhD from the University of California, Berkeley.

DR. JOAN WAUGH is Professor of History at the University of California at Los Angeles. Her most recent book is entitled *U. S. Grant: American Hero, American Myth* (2009), and her other books include *Unsentimental Reformer: The Life of Josephine Shaw Lowell* (1997); *The Memory of the Civil War in American Culture* (coedited with Alice Fahs, 2004); and *Wars within a War: Controversy and Conflict over the American Civil War* (coedited with Gary W. Gallagher, 2009). She received her BA, MA, and PhD from the University of California at Los Angeles.

Books by Conference Participants

Ayers, Edward L. *In the Presence of Mine Enemies: Civil War in the Heart of America.* New York: Norton, 2003.

———. *The Promise of the New South: Life After Reconstruction.* New York: Oxford University Press, 1992.

———. *What Caused the Civil War? Reflections on the South and Southern History.* New York: Norton, 2005.

Baker, Jean H. *Mary Todd Lincoln: A Biography.* New York: Norton, 1987.

———. *Sisters: The Lives of America's Suffragists.* New York: Hill and Wang, 2005.

Baker, Jean H., David Herbert Donald, and Michael Holt. *The Civil War and Reconstruction.* New York: Norton, 2001.

Blight, David W. *Race and Reunion: The Civil War in American Memory.* Cambridge, Mass.: Belknap Press of Harvard University Press, 2001.

———. *A Slave No More: Two Men Who Escaped to Freedom, Including Their Own Narratives of Emancipation.* New York: Harcourt, 2007.

Crofts, Daniel W. *Old Southampton: Politics and Society in a Virginia County, 1834–1869.* Charlottesville: University Press of Virginia, 1992.

———. *Reluctant Confederates: Upper South Unionists in the Secession Crisis.* Chapel Hill: University of North Carolina Press, 1989.

Dew, Charles B. *Apostles of Disunion: Southern Secession Commissioners and the Causes of the Civil War.* Charlottesville: University Press of Virginia, 2001.

———. *Bond of Iron: Master and Slave at Buffalo Forge.* New York: Norton, 1994.

———. *Ironmaker to the Confederacy: Joseph R. Anderson and the Tredegar Iron Works.* Richmond: Library of Virginia, 1999.

Gallagher, Gary W. *Causes Won, Lost, and Forgotten: How Hollywood and Popular Art Shape What We Know about the Civil War.* Chapel Hill: University of North Carolina Press, 2008.

———. *The Confederate War.* Cambridge, Mass.: Harvard University Press, 1997.

———. *Lee and His Generals in War and Memory.* Baton Rouge: Louisiana State University Press, 1998.

Johnson, Walter. *Soul by Soul: Life Inside the Antebellum Slave Market.* Cambridge, Mass.: Harvard University Press, 1999.

Kenzer, Robert C. *Enterprising Southerners: Black Economic Success in North Carolina, 1865–1915.* Charlottesville: University Press of Virginia, 1997.

———. *Kinship and Neighborhood in a Southern Community: Orange County, North Carolina, 1849–1881.* Knoxville: University of Tennessee Press, 1987.

Kenzer, Robert C., and John C. Inscoe, eds. *Enemies of My Country: New Perspectives on Unionists in the Civil War South.* Athens: University of Georgia Press, 2001.

Kimball, Gregg D. *American City, Southern Place: A Cultural History of Antebellum Richmond.* Athens: University of Georgia Press, 2000.

Lankford, Nelson D. *Cry Havoc! The Crooked Road to Civil War, 1861.* New York: Viking, 2007.

———. *Richmond Burning: The Last Days of the Confederate Capital.* New York: Viking, 2002.

———, ed. *The Virginia Magazine of History and Biography.* Richmond: Virginia Historical Society, published quarterly.

Lankford, Nelson D., and Charles F. Bryan Jr. *Eye of the Storm: A Civil War Odyssey.* New York: Free Press, 2000.

Lee, Lauranett L. *Making the American Dream Work: A Cultural History of African Americans in Hopewell, Virginia.* Garden City, NY: Morgan James Publishing, 2008.

Reynolds, David S. *John Brown, Abolitionist: The Man Who Killed Slavery, Sparked the Civil War, and Seeded Civil Rights.* New York: Alfred A. Knopf, 2005.

———. *Waking Giant: America in the Age of Jackson.* New York: Harper, 2008.

Sinha, Manisha. *The Counterrevolution of Slavery: Politics and Ideology in Antebellum South Carolina.* Chapel Hill: University of North Carolina Press, 2000.

Sinha, Manisha, and John H. Bracey, eds. *African American Mosaic: A Documentary History from the Slave Trade to the Twenty First Century.* 2 vols. Upper Saddle River, NJ: Pearson Prentice Hall, 2004.

Sinha, Manisha, and Penny Von Eschen, eds. *Contested Democracy: Freedom, Race and Power in American History.* New York: Columbia University Press, 2007.

Varon, Elizabeth R. *Disunion! The Coming of the American Civil War, 1789–1859.* Littlefield History of the Civil War Era series, vol. 1. Chapel Hill: University of North Carolina Press, 2008.

———. *Southern Lady, Yankee Spy: The True Story of Elizabeth Van Lew, A Union Agent in the Heart of the Confederacy.* New York: Oxford University Press, 2003.

———. *We Mean to Be Counted: White Women and Politics in Antebellum Virginia.* Chapel Hill: University of North Carolina Press, 1998.

Walker, Clarence E. *Deromanticizing Black History: Critical Essays and Reappraisals.* Knoxville: University of Tennessee Press, 1991.

———. *Mongrel Nation: The America Begotten By Thomas Jefferson and Sally Hemings.* Charlottesville: University of Virginia Press, 2009.

———. *A Rock in a Weary Land: The African Methodist Episcopal Church During the Civil War and Reconstruction.* Baton Rouge: Louisiana State University Press, 1982.

———. *We Can't Go Home Again: An Argument about Afrocentrism.* New York: Oxford University Press, 2001.

Walker, Clarence E., and Gregory D. Smithers. *The Preacher and the Politician: Jeremiah Wright, Barack Obama, and Race in America.* Charlottesville: University of Virginia Press, 2009.

Waugh, Joan. *Unsentimental Reformer: The Life of Josephine Shaw Lowell.* Cambridge, Mass.: Harvard University Press, 1997.

———. *U. S. Grant: American Hero, American Myth.* Chapel Hill: University of North Carolina Press, 2009.

Waugh, Joan, and Alice Fahs, eds. *The Memory of the Civil War in American Culture.* Chapel Hill: University of North Carolina Press, 2004.

Waugh, Joan, and Gary W. Gallagher, eds. *Wars within a War: Controversy and Conflict over the American Civil War.* Chapel Hill: University of North Carolina Press, 2009.

INDEX

Italicized page numbers refer to illustrations.